The Way of the Emigrants

Badawi and Catherine Simon in America

Louis Farshee

authorHOUSE®

AuthorHouse™
1663 Liberty Drive
Bloomington, IN 47403
www.authorhouse.com
Phone: 1-800-839-8640

First published by AuthorHouse 2/22/2010

ISBN: 978-1-4490-4773-3 (e)
ISBN: 978-1-4490-4771-9 (sc)
ISBN: 978-1-4490-4772-6 (hc)

Library of Congress Control Number: 2009912275

Printed in the United States of America
Bloomington, Indiana

This book is printed on acid-free paper.

"…not one of the minutes we live would have existed without the thousands of years which have preceeded it since the Creation, and not one of our heart-beats would have been possible had it not been for the successive generations of ancestors…"

From: *The Rock of Tanios* by Amin Maalouf

Contents

Preface

I never had the opportunity to know Badawi and Catherine Simon, my paternal grandparents. They were no longer living when I was born. Over time, the combination of their absence and my curiosity led me to ask questions about them. Sometimes I posed questions to my father, George Farshee, the youngest of the Simon children. Of the many answers I heard the one I never quite understood at the time was the different surnames used by the same family. Why Farchakh, Farshee, Forshee and Simon? Another source of confusion was our ethnic heritage. When I was a child we were Syrians but in later years we became Lebanese. What was this all about, I asked myself? It wasn't until some years had passed did I learn the answers to these questions.

During one of our conversations in the 1970s, my father suggested that with my apparent interest in our family's history I should research the lives of his parents and perhaps write a book. I told him it was an interesting idea but did little until 1981. That year, I learned that a cousin from Lebanon, Paul Farchakh, was attending college in Los Angeles. When Paul and I met in person, we talked nonstop for fifteen hours. Throughout the years that I have worked intermittently on this project, he has contributed considerable information and suggestions.

In the almost three decades that have passed since our first meeting, Paul has become a husband, father, educator and established artist living in Lebanon and he continues to extend his help, reading the final manuscript before it was submitted for publication.

After my father met Paul and had some of his own questions answered, he said that I should get serious about my project and begin interviewing various relatives who, by this time, were getting up in years. I began my research within weeks but some relatives were already gone. Of the six Farshee children, the oldest, Aziz Farshee, had died when I was eight years old, and I barely remember him. The next two, Mary Simon Azar and Johnny Farshee, I knew during my adolescence but had never asked them any questions about family history. I was more fortunate with the three youngest, Sy Forshee, Frances Simon Miaoulis, and my father, who were living well into my adult years.

My first interviews were conducted in the US. In September 1981 I spent a weekend in Jacksonville, Florida with my uncle Sy Forshee and his wife Addie. Addie had known the Simon family some years before marrying Sy, having been a neighbor. She was very helpful. Sy knew a great deal about his parent's history and shared many stories and anecdotes with me. He also suggested certain questions that should be answered. My aunt, Frances Simon Miaoulis, located a large envelope in her Montgomery, Alabama home that contained a number of original documents pertaining to her father and several photographs of his siblings. She had her father's Bible which included a page detailing the birth and baptism (and two deaths) of the Simon children. During the early phase of my inquiries Frances was my co-researcher. She traveled with me to Mobile and Birmingham where cousins and others were interviewed.

I expanded my travels and inquiries to Mexico, France and Lebanon in 1982. In January I traveled to Mexico City to meet Paul's uncle, George Farchakh, who I knew of but had never met. His wife, Salma, a UNESCO translator, was attending a conference in Mexico City and we decided to meet there. From Mexico City, George and I traveled by bus to Puebla to visit and interview members of the Nakad family and a man named Maroun Brahim. Later that year, George and Salma hosted me in their Paris suburb home. George has the journal of our great-grandfather, Semaan Mkhayel Farchakh, and in it he found answers to a number of my questions.

In October 1982, I made my first of nearly a dozen trips to Lebanon. Aside from the fact that the Civil War was in its seventh year, the trip had a powerful emotional impact on me. I was the first Farchakh relative from the US to return to Lebanon in sixty-one years and the welcome I received was remarkable. In addition to meeting dozens of cousins whose contributions are listed in the bibliography and family friends too numerous to list, the history of my grandparents came to life when I saw their first apartment in the old part of the town of Zgharta. The places to which I traveled, the interviews that were conducted, and the documents and other sources that were studied became the story that is told in *The Way of the Emigrants*.

Badawi Simon 1915

Catherine Simon 1928

Prologue:
Friday, November 14, 1924

A Model T Ford traveling south of Montgomery, Alabama near the small community of Dublin turned off Carter Hill Road into the driveway of Joe Money's home. Immediately off the road was an accumulation of loose sand, and, when the wheels hit it, the car suddenly stopped. Those sitting on the porch of the Money home located about a hundred yards from the highway saw all this happen. Expecting the driver to restart the engine and proceed to the house, they waited for a short time but nothing happened. Roused by their curiosity, they began walking to the car. Someone called out to the driver but there was no answer. Stepping up to the side of the car they peered through the window and saw its only occupant slumped over the steering wheel. They called his name but there was no reply. Doctor Bernard Simon was dead.[1]

Fifty-two year old Doctor Simon was a well-known optometrist who traveled from Montgomery to communities in South Alabama to make house calls and perform eye examinations. His usual routine included visiting individual patients and sometimes making arrangements to set up his optician's trial case in a friend's home, a hotel lobby, or grocery store. For extended trips, he usually spent nights with families he knew from his business dealings.

Earlier that week there were indications that Doctor Simon was not well, but symptoms pointing to a possible heart attack were misunderstood or misdiagnosed. On Wednesday he had complained of indigestion. The next day, after visiting his long-time friend Assad Barad, he was expected home in time for supper. Some time after he should have arrived and was seemingly not there his wife happened to walk past a bedroom and discovered him lying across the bed. Knowing he did not take afternoon naps, she sensed something was wrong and asked if he was ill. He told her he thought he had an upset stomach.[2]

On Friday, the day of his death, Doctor Simon and his wife Catherine drove to the home of their eldest daughter and her husband, Mary and Zaki Azar to join them for lunch. The Simons lived about a block and a half from the Azars and could have walked the short distance, but Doctor Simon planned to leave from there to keep his appointment in Dublin. Catherine stayed after her husband's departure to spend part of the afternoon with Mary and the children. Zaki returned to his downtown store. In mid-afternoon Doctor Simon departed the Azar home and stopped en route at a drug store where he told a pharmacist friend he had an upset stomach. He purchased a soda powder formulation, returned to his car and continued his trip. As far as is known, his conversation with the pharmacist was the last time anyone spoke with Doctor Simon.[3]

Dr. Bernard Simon, Optometrist, as his business card read, was the adopted and professional name of a naturalized Syrian immigrant named Badawi Semaan Farchakh, pronounced *Bad'-we Sim-ahn' Far'-shockh* in the distinctive accent of his old country village.[4] His story and that of his wife and their US family began several thousand miles from the sandy driveway on Carter Hill Road in that part of Syria known throughout history as Mount Lebanon. Badawi was born there in the village of Ehden in 1873.[5]

He grew to adulthood in Ehden and its companion village Zgharta. In 1890, at age seventeen, he married his sixteen-year-old sweetheart, Khaltoum Khoury. Within a few months they immigrated to the US with a group of friends and relatives and began their family in New Orleans, Louisiana, when Catherine, as Khaltoum came to be known, gave birth to a boy in 1893. Fourteen months later, their first daughter was born in Jacksonville, Florida. In 1897 the Simon family returned to Lebanon where they stayed for about two years. During that time, their third child, a son, was born. A second immigration was made to the US in 1899 where they all lived for the remainder of their lives. Many events filled their years, some joyous some sad, but the starting point of their story was in Mount Lebanon when it and all of Syria was a province of the Ottoman Empire.

Ehden, Zgharta and Religious Heritage

Ehden, where Badawi Simon was born, is an ancient village with a history going back to at least the time of the Canaanites, a Semitic people the Greeks named Phoenicians.[1] Today, traveling there by car from Tripoli, one proceeds in a generally southeasterly direction on a road that twists and turns for a distance of about twenty miles. From Ehden, situated in the heartland of Mount Lebanon at an altitude of 4920 feet above sea level, one can see much of North Lebanon, some of southwest Syria and, under favorable weather conditions, the island of Cyprus 70 miles west of Lebanon's coast. The picturesque village whose name translates as Eden sits on a hilly limestone shelf amid trees and springs overlooking the craggy steep cliffs of the *Wadi Qadisha,* the Holy Valley. This geologic spectacle with its breathtaking colors and rock formations is a steep-sided gorge where holy men and hermits lived from the earliest of Christian times. Except on some summer weekends when the village is crowded, Ehden is a quiet little place. In times of civil strife, it has proved to be a refuge protected by mountains and the Holy Valley making it accessible by only one road from the plain below.

Wintertime brings snow to Ehden that can sometimes accumulate to a depth of ten feet or more, but between May and September it is a village in motion. Outdoor social activities center around the *midan*, the main square with a host of coffee shops, open-air restaurants, sweet shops and miscellaneous commercial establishments. In the summer time villagers and visitors go there to socialize, drink coffee or dine under the pollution-free sky that at night is a purple canopy filled with countless stars. The air is cool, the humidity low and there are no flying insects. Immediately adjacent to the *midan* is the old *souk* or market with a butcher shop and a variety of small family owned stores. Waterfalls and streams are plentiful and a short distance from the heart of the village is *Horsh Ehden*, the Ehden Forest, one of Lebanon's nature preserves and a place of beauty with numerous varieties of plants, trees, birds, and other animal life.

Architecture tells much of the story of this old village with homes and other structures reflecting traditional Lebanese, Byzantine, Ottoman, and contemporary influences. Some have been modified over the years with a patchwork of materials and styles that suggest more than one architectural influence. Nowhere is the contrast of centuries more dramatic than when one sees the two churches that sit above Ehden on the western pinnacle of Mount Saydet. The smallest, over a thousand years old, is said to have been built of stone recovered from the ruins of a Canaanite temple and is revered as *Saydet el Hosn*, Our Lady of the Fortress. This little place of worship is unique among Ehden's other churches because it is a shrine to the Virgin Mary, the patroness of the village. Centuries of tradition are traversed a few steps from the old stone church where a much larger and modern cathedral of cement and steel was dedicated in 1989. Its belfry and cross towers above all the structures of Ehden and can be seen for many miles from the surrounding lands.

Until recently, Ehden was largely unpopulated in the winter and left to the care of a keeper who patrolled and guarded the village. Today, many of the historical structures have been restored and the *midan* modernized based largely on ideas proposed by environmental architect Pierre Farchakh in the early 1980s. A few of the main roads have been widened and a bypass constructed around the town. Ehden remains the summer home of families from Zgharta but has become a resort town for visitors and tourists. Television satellite dishes can be seen on many structures, and part of its transformation has resulted in a commercial infrastructure that includes several hotels and a country club.[2]

Early on the people of Ehden did not remain within the confines of their village. Gradually, they spread throughout the mountains in all directions and began to populate the lands below. Just north of the Koura plateau near the traditional western boundary of Mount Lebanon and about five miles southeast of Tripoli, they built the village of Zgharta. Although Zgharta and Ehden are about fourteen miles apart, they are governed as a single municipality and share the same population. One explanation for the two villages with a single population is said to have occurred several hundred years ago. A nobleman and his men traveling in the mountains during the winter found themselves trapped in a sudden snow storm. The people of Ehden invited the nobleman and his soldiers into their homes and provided shelter for their animals. In gratitude for their life-saving hospitality, the nobleman promised the people they would not have to endure another winter in the mountains. He prevailed upon the Ottoman government to cede to them the "land between the rivers," an area on the plain below bounded on one side by the Joueit River which begins in the Ehden Forest and the Rachiin River on the other.[3] Before flowing into the Mediterranean at Tripoli, they converge to form the Abu Ali River. Nearby is Ardat, the Ardata of ancient history that flourished around 1450 B.C. This is the site of Zgharta, a name of obscure origin understood by some to mean "It is too small."

At about 500 feet above sea level, Zgharta lies at a lower elevation than Ehden and covers a series of gently rolling hills. In time, the people of Ehden built homes there and cultivated the land with vegetables and groves of olive trees and later with orchards of oranges, lemons, and pomegranates. Because of their valor and uncompromising defense of their homes and land, the people of Ehden and Zgharta are referred to as lions, an age-old Middle East metaphor for gallant men and women. The twin communities of Ehden and Zgharta are each known as a "village of lions." The Zghartawis, as they are called, have pride in their two towns. To them the villages that dot the winding road going up to Ehden are not situated "above Zgharta" but, rather, "below Ehden."

In succeeding centuries, the people of Zgharta left their "winter" homes for the journey to Ehden on the Sunday Maronite Christians know as the Feast of the Resurrection, Easter Sunday. They lived there throughout the summer tending their apple orchards and cultivating gardens often terraced on mountain sides and valley walls. Terraces were constructed over a long period of time and continue to be built today. Their purpose is to extend the arable land and protect the soil against erosion. From a distance some of them look like stair steps for giants. At the end of the growing season, crops were harvested and about the time of the first frost the people packed up their belongings and returned to Zgharta.

Badawi and Catherine Simon their families and ancestors were born into the Maronite Church, the dominant Christian rite in Mount Lebanon. The Maronites did not originate in Lebanon but in the Syrian hinterland by the followers of a 5th century holy man named Saint Maroun.

Depending upon which historian one cites, the Maronites arrived in the mountains of Lebanon between the 5th and 11th centuries. Some contemporary historians such as Kamal Salibi and Fawwaz Traboulsi place the migration to Mount Lebanon around the year 1000. There is no consensus as to the time they emerged in Mount Lebanon and the expanse of dates might be attributable to the fact that the migration did not occur all at once but took place over an extended period of time.

Some of the details pertaining to Maronite history are speculative at best. Numerous writers have made assorted claims, many of which are not supported by any documentation. Arguably the most widely accepted account of the emergence of the Maronites in Mount Lebanon is the traditional one cited by Maronite Church historian Bishop Pierre Dib. Based upon the research and writings of earlier historians, Bishop Dib wrote that the Maronites began their migration from northern Syria in the 6th century. It came about after the massacre of 350 Maronite monks by heretical Jacobite Christians and the Jacobite destruction of many Maronite monasteries. The exact year in which *the* Monastery of Saint Maroun located in Syria's Orontes Valley near Apameus was destroyed is speculative since certain other documents Bishop Dib cites places the event in the first half of the tenth century. This is the same timeframe presented by Salibi and Traboulsi.

A second explanation posits that the Maronites were the same people who were known as the *Jurajima*, a group of fierce Syrian fighters. They were deployed into Mount Lebanon by the Byzantine Empire as a bulwark against the expanding Arab Caliphate Empire that had conquered Damascus and most of Syria in 636. This theory too is fraught with disagreement among historians who debate over questions such as who the *Jurajima* were and the geographical location of their origin.

Finally, there is the theory favored by researcher Matti Moosa who bases his revisionist views on the absence of any historical evidence that meets his standards. He contends that there was no Maronite migration from the Syrian hinterland. Rather, they were originally part of the indigenous Syrian Orthodox religious community already living in Mount Lebanon and were converted through the efforts of Maronite missionaries from northern Syria.

Regardless of the exact date of their arrival, there is credible evidence that the Maronites were living in the mountains of North Lebanon by the 8th century. The first Maronite church, the Church of *Mar* (Saint) Mema, named for an early Greek saint spelled variously Memas, Memah or Memmah, was erected in Ehden in 749 on the ruins of a Roman sun temple. The restored church is today a well-known landmark. As a religious group, the Maronites were originally part of the Byzantine Church but the two groups split in 680-681. The Maronites remained a separate confessional group until they recognized the supremacy of the pope in the 12th century and, in the early 18th century, entered into a concordant with Rome. Certain Maronite practices were Latinized over time, but they maintained their traditional liturgy and their own corpus of canon law. Bishops are elected to office independently of Rome and they in turn elect their patriarch. This office was created in 685, a couple of years after the Maronite break with the Byzantine Church, when the first patriarch, Saint John Maroun, not to be confused with Saint Maroun, the 5th century saint, became the first patriarch. After the Vatican II council (1962-1965), the Maronite patriarch along with other Eastern Rite patriarchs was accorded the rank of cardinal in the Roman Catholic Church.

Entering into formal union with Rome did not change some of the rules of Maronite priesthood. Men who become priests may be married prior to ordination. This tradition is not extended to lands where the Latin Rite is dominant and Maronite priests in those jurisdictions must remain celibate. Marriage among lay persons is permitted between first cousins in contrast to the Latin Church which prohibits marriages closer than third-degree kinship.

Old Names and New Names

In any story about people, the characters have assigned names. This conventional method of identification, however, as it applies to this story is not as simple as it might appear. Family names change and it is not unusual for certain individuals to be known by more than one given name.

According to historian Philip Hitti, family names in Lebanon originated in the late 11th century at about the time of the First Crusade. A man might identify himself (in Arabic) as *"ana Louis ahl al jubal,"* that is, "I am Louis, a person of the mountain." By dropping the attributive, *al jubal*, this example name becomes Louis Ahl.[1] Wide use of the Ahl surname became a source of confusion in Church and land records. To differentiate between diverse "Ahl" families alternate names began to be used. They came from a number of different sources such as a person's trade, vocation, physical characteristic, place of origin, or nickname. From the almost limitless lexicon of nicknames, Farchakh as a family name came into use.

Farchakh does not translate into a single English word but has several meanings related to the position of a man's legs. It may mean a man who sits with his knees apart or takes long steps or perhaps jumps a great distance by widely extending his legs. According to sources in Lebanon, the Farchakh name originated with an 18th century ancestor named Badawi Ahl. This particular Badawi, not to be confused with the Badawi Simon of our story, was described as a big man in stature who was the *nazzar* or superintendent of a silk mill near Zgharta. Because he sat with his knees apart his fellow workers dubbed him *el Farchakh Badawi*, the wide-kneed Badawi. The nickname stuck and over time Badawi Ahl became known as Badawi Farchakh.

When Badawi's son Mkhayel (Michael) was born in the early 19th century, he was known as Mkhayel Badawi Farchakh. Among his three sons was Semaan Mkhayel (Simon Michael) Farchakh, the father of Badawi Semaan Farchakh, the Badawi Simon of this story. After immigrating to the US, Badawi Semaan Farchakh became Badawi Simon. He did not use his Lebanese surname. Excluding his death certificate and obituary where he was identified in both by incorrect spellings of Farshee, the family name eventually adopted by his sons, all other known documents refer to him as Badawi Simon or simply B. Simon. Around 1916, while transforming himself from an itinerant peddler into a practicing optometrist, he began to use the name Bernard Simon.[2]

Given names may also be confusing to those unfamiliar with Middle Eastern traditions and are often used repetitively within a family. As a general rule but not always, a man's first son is named after the boy's paternal grandfather. If a Christian child's first name is a traditional Arabic name, for example, *Aziz* (m), *Azizi* (f), *Jamil* (m), *Jamili* (f), *Said* (m), *Saidi* (f), etc., he or she might be given a Christian name at the time of baptism. Badawi Simon's children all had two given names, a traditional Arabic name and a baptismal name.[3] The traditional Arabic and Christian names were not used together; rather, the child or adult was known by one or the other.

The Simon children, boys and girls, all had the same middle name. They might have been known by either their traditional or baptismal first name, but it was followed by *Badawi*. This ordering of names was and continues to be a tradition practiced throughout the Middle East. The identifiers *ibn* (son of) and *bint* (daughter of) between a child's given name and his or her father's name is usually omitted in Lebanese names. If it is not present it is assumed. This tradition not only identifies the child's father for legal and religious purposes, it serves as a means of differentiating members of an extended family who carry the same given name. For example, the most popular given name among Farchakh men in Lebanon is Sarkis. To keep them separate and identify which Sarkis one is referring to, he might be referred to as Sarkis [son of] Semaan, Sarkis [son of] Boutros, Sarkis [son of] Youssef, etc.

The tradition of addressing an adult is also at variance with Western etiquette. In most Arabic-speaking societies, adults are not addressed as Mr. or Mrs. or by their first names but by an Arabic epithet known as the *kunyah* designation, *Abu* (father of) or *Umm* (mother of), followed by the name of their oldest son. This is not a formal salutation such as Sir or Madam but a gesture of propriety and respect. As this applies to Badawi and Catherine Simon, they would have been known among their old country friends and relations as *Abu Aziz* and *Umm Aziz*. Children address their parents by various versions of "father" and "mother" as children do everywhere. While some kinship names such as *sitti* and *jiddo*, grandmother and grandfather, apply to both paternal and maternal grandparents, most others are more specific. Uncles and aunts are identified and addressed by nouns that convey exact kinship such as *ame*, "my father's brother," *mart ame*, "my father's brother's wife," *amte*, "my father's sister," etc.

In the Simon family, some of Badawi and Catherine's children were known by their baptismal name while others were known by their traditional given name. The use of a particular given name seems to have been linked to the moment in time when acquaintances and friendships began. Old country friends and relatives who knew the Simon children before they began using baptismal names addressed them by the traditional names while non-family members and newer acquaintances usually used the baptismal names. This is a general observation, not a hard and fast rule. In the US, the ordering of names, i.e., given name followed by the father's first name, was not used by any of Badawi and Catherine's children in the naming of their respective children.

Badawi's wife presents yet another aspect in the development of names. Her maiden name was Khaltoum Joseph Tarek, Joseph being her father's name. Like the Farchakhs, the Tareks originated in Ehden.[4] The surname Tarek, also like Farchakh, is a nickname and is derived from the Arabic verb, *taraka*, to hit. Assigning Tarek as a nickname suggests one who in a confrontation was inclined to hit first and debate later. To further complicate matters, Khaltoum's grandfather, Elias Khoury, was a Maronite priest. The Arabic word for priest preceded by the definite article is *el khoury*. After his ordination, Elias Tarek became known as Elias Khoury and the name of his vocation became his family name. The article *el*, applicable to most Arabic family names, is not always used.

Khaltoum is a traditional Arabic name which means "peace" or "happiness," but, in the US, she was known to friends and acquaintances as Catherine. According to their children, Badawi addressed her as Khaltoum or a diminutive form, Katool.[5] Whether Catherine was Khaltoum's baptismal name or an adopted name has not been determined.

Badawi and Catherine

There are scant details relating to Badawi Simon's formative years growing up in Zgharta and Ehden. The degree of formal education his father Semaan Mkhayel Farchakh was able to provide young Badawi and the other children is uncertain although the Jesuits had established a school next to Our Lady of Zgharta Church in the 18th century, and, later, the French Lazarist fathers opened one in the middle of the 19th century.[1] Badawi was literate in Arabic, but any proficiency he might have had in other languages while growing up in Mount Lebanon is not known. In the US, he was fluent in English and spoke with a very slight accent. Catherine's spoken English was heavily accented.[2]

In his formative years, young Badawi heard stories from his uncle, another man with the name Badawi, about his immigration to the US some years earlier. The uncle returned to Mount Lebanon with money he used to purchase land, and among the gifts he brought were several Winchester rifles.[3] Throughout his life, Badawi Simon adhered to the teachings of the Maronite faith and was devoted to the Virgin Mary. He always carried a rosary in one of his pockets. In personal appearance he was a handsome, well-dressed young man of pleasant demeanor who preferred wearing silk shirts and sometimes sported a fashionable walking stick. In fact, according to one source who knew him in the old country, he was known as a "dude" because of his dapper dress.[4] His penchant for fashionable attire and silk shirts led him to his wife-to-be who, with her sisters, was a seamstress who made silk garments.

Catherine Khoury's most distinguishing physical feature was her green eyes. She was of modest height with black curly hair. Her parents died within two weeks of each other from a fever in 1881 when Catherine was seven years old. There were four Khoury daughters, and Catherine was raised by her older sisters. When she reminisced about the old country, she would tell her children about the outings she and her sisters would take when they traveled from Zgharta to Tripoli and boarded the southbound train for the ten mile trip to Chekka. Here the Khoury sisters swam and picnicked on the sandy beaches of El Herri under the blue skies of the Mediterranean. One sister, Mary, married Salim Isaac Nakad from Kfardlakous, a village adjacent to Zgharta. Another died at sea. According to the story Catherine told, this sister, whose name has been forgotten, married a Lebanese merchant, and, together, they immigrated to South America. After a few years, the husband wanted to return to Lebanon but at the time his wife, Catherine's sister, was not in good health. The husband insisted that the journey be made according to his wishes, and when they departed she was still in bad health. While at sea she died. Rather than pay for the special handling of his deceased wife's body and returning it to Lebanon for a traditional burial, the husband had her buried at sea. Catherine loathed her brother-in-law for what he had done. The episode troubled her because she believed that the burial at sea would prevent her sister's resurrection for the Final Judgment.[5]

When she and Badawi married in 1890 at *Saydet Zgharta*, Our Lady of Zgharta, the newlyweds made a pilgrimage to the Cedars of Lebanon, known in Arabic as *Arz el Rab*, Cedars of God. At the time, a fallen cedar tree had been maneuvered and placed against a cliff by an old hermit-priest and keeper who lived in the forest. Water from a spring on the mountainside poured through the hollowed log to the ground below. Badawi climbed the cliff and brought Catherine water from its source.[6] At first glance, this gesture might be seen as a romantic episode but there was another implication. Making pilgrimages to ancient trees and gushing springs had a religious significance and is a tradition that has endured for thousands of years in the Middle East. Displays of nature were thought to be manifestations of supernatural presence and influence. Pilgrimages by Christians, Muslims and Druze in Lebanon, Syria and Palestine to sites such as *Arz el Rab* date from antiquity.[7] While at the Cedars, Badawi and Catherine collected a small amount of earth to take with them to the New World, a practice common among emigrants as they prepared to depart their homeland.

Although Catherine has now been dead the better part of a century, it is still possible to catch a glimpse of the person she was through various stories that circulated among the family. Some are still told today in Lebanon. To those who knew and admired her, she was described as a "steel-minded" woman who asserted herself when she deemed it appropriate to do so. Conversely, to those who did not admire her traits of individuality, she was probably considered stubborn or obstinate. An early example of her resolve is found in a story that occurred shortly after her marriage. She and Badawi had taken an apartment in what is today Old Zgharta in a building that still stands. Prior to their marriage, Badawi had a beard which Catherine seemingly tolerated. One Sunday morning, she put on her most tattered dress in preparation for church. When questioned by her husband if she intended to wear it to church, she told him that until he shaved his beard she would. Some discussion ensued but ended when Badawi agreed to shave his beard. There must have been some degree of compromise because she didn't get her way entirely. He left a full mustache. They proceeded to church with Catherine wearing more appropriate attire.[8]

On another occasion in their early US days, she was traveling with Badawi on his peddler's route. It was not unusual for wives to work side by side with their husbands on these forays, nor was it unusual for Syrian women to work alone as peddlers although Catherine never did. On this particular day, it was summertime in South Alabama, and the weather was hot and humid. They stopped at a rural grocery store and asked the owner for drinking water. The man accommodated their request and brought them water in a glass pitcher. Before giving it to them, he demanded a price of ten cents. Catherine wasn't too happy about being coerced into buying water but paid the man nonetheless. She and Badawi leisurely drank the water. After they finished, she proceeded to pack the pitcher in Badawi's *qashe* (also spelled *kashshi*), his merchandise case. When the grocer realized what was going on, he became irate and insisted that the pitcher be returned to him. Catherine resolutely explained that, because water came from God, the ten cents must have been the price of the pitcher. She held her ground and kept the pitcher as she and Badawi continued their trek.[9]

Those who remembered her said she had a quick sense of humor and an equally quick temper. She was a woman not to be trifled with and had no reluctance to stand her ground. According to a story that occurred during the Mobile years, she and Badawi were sitting around their kitchen table having coffee with their long-time friend, Sarkis Maroni. Their friendship went back to the old country, and his wife Mary was a daughter of one of Badawi's aunts. Sarkis was a friendly, good-hearted man known for his humorous observations. The table talk turned to an exchange about the shortcomings associated with being a route peddler. As the conversation proceeded, Sarkis made a passing comment that one of those shortcomings might be *Umm Aziz* being tempted to "fool around" when Badawi was traveling on business. About the time the two men began to chuckle, Catherine came up out of her chair and threw her half-filled cup of coffee into Sarkis's face. Laughter stopped and a few tense moments followed before Sarkis apologized profusely while wiping coffee from his face and clothes. Over a period of years, the long-time friend continued to be a regular visitor to the Simon home, but he never again made any remarks about the temptations of *Umm Aziz*.[10]

Catherine's personality and temperament was, in some ways, the exact opposite of Badawi's. He too is said to have had a temper but was described as a somewhat more unflappable individual and considerably less explosive than his wife. She once observed that her husband would rather "jump in the lake" than get into an argument. Different personalities or not, Badawi and Catherine's children consistently said that they never heard a cross word between them.[11]

The Old Country Family

Badawi Simon's father, Semaan Mkhayel (Simon Michael) Farchakh, was born in 1839,[1] his mother Warda (Rose), about 1850. Semaan was the middle son of Mkhayel Badawi Farchakh, the oldest son being Badawi Mkhayel, the youngest Tannous Mkhayel.[2] Warda was one of the daughters of the Zedda family who, along with members of other families from Ehden, had married into the Farchakh family. One of Warda's sisters, Samira, sometimes referred to by her baptismal name, Theresa, married Jabbour Lawoun Karam. From this union came five children, four boys and one girl. Among them were sons Assad and Mansour. In the US, Mansour Jabbour Lawoun Karam occasionally used the surname Lawon or Lawoun, but the family name he and his brother Assad eventually settled on was Leon.[4]

Another US family whose kinship to the Farchakhs goes back to the old country is the Soto (originally Soutou) family of Mobile through a sister of Semaan Mkhayel named Warda, not to be confused with Semaan Mkhayel's wife also named Warda. To keep these two Wardas separate, Semaan Mkhayel's sister is referred to as *Warda Mkhayel*. *Warda Mkhayel* married Boutros (Peter) Soutou and together they were parents to a son, Hanna (John) and a daughter, Selima, Anglicized as

Selma. In the matter of kinship, the children of the following couples were first cousins: Semaan Mkhayel Farchakh and Warda Zedda, Boutros Soutou and *Warda Mkhayel* Farchakh, and Jabbour Lawon Karam and Samira (Theresa) Zedda.[5]

Various stories circulated in the US from some of the Simon's old country friends and relatives who described Semaan Mkhayel Farchakh as a man of princely wealth. Those stories contended that he owned an olive grove that was so vast it required the labor of 80-100 workers to harvest. His home in Ehden was constructed of stone with marble floors and had columns that supported the front roof. His land holdings were so extensive that a herd of cows could not traverse it in a single day. And, as if all this was not enough to establish his fortune he reportedly owned a silk mill.[6]

It is difficult to determine what if any part of these stories is factual. For example, having a home in Lebanon constructed of stone with marble floors is not an indication of princely wealth. A structure of this type might be unusual in the US, but it was not then and is not now a rarity in Lebanon. Stone and marble are preferred materials for home construction due largely to the limited availability of wood. But the description given of Semaan Mkhayel's home is strikingly similar to the one seen today when they visit the home of Youssef Bey Karam[7] in Ehden. The house is constructed of stone, has marble floors, columns, and the pink color is the same as that described in the "princely wealth" stories. No other house in Ehden dating from the 19th century looks like Youssef Bey's.

Among the other possessions of the Karam family was a silk mill and extensive landholdings. At the moment in time assigned to the "wealth" stories, the 1880s, Youssef Bey was living in exile in Italy, and it is reasonable to believe that Semaan Mkhayel might have been overseeing his property and holdings. If this premise is accurate, the assets attributed to Semaan Mkhayel Farchakh were not his but belonged to Youssef Bey Karam or the Karam family. Semaan Mkhayel was indeed a landowner, but most of the stories about his personal wealth are conjecture, immigrant myth or perhaps hyperbole.

If there was an element of confusion about the ownership of property it might attributable to the relationship between the Karams and Farchakhs. During the latter part of the nineteenth century, the two families were very close. Their ties went back to at least the time when Semaan Mkhayel fought alongside Youssef Bey and acted in an intelligence gathering capacity during Karam's quest for Lebanon's independence.[8] Karam's uprising had its roots in events that occurred in 1860 which contributed to the emigration of the peasant class from Mount Lebanon.

That year, civil war erupted in Mount Lebanon between Maronites and Druze. The fighting resulted in the massacre of twelve-thousand Christians and soon spread to Damascus where more Christians were massacred under the complicit eyes of the local Ottoman administration.[9] Officials from Constantinople (Istanbul) restored order and punished many of those responsible for the killings.[10] Nonetheless, Napoleon III of France dispatched an expeditionary corps that landed in Beirut. In an attempt to settle the dispute and prevent a reoccurrence, European powers led by France and Great Britain persuaded Constantinople to declare parts of Mount Lebanon a semi-autonomous enclave under the administration of a Christian governor.[11] Although Karam was instrumental in ending an earlier Peasant's Revolt which began in 1858 he was passed over for the post, and, much to his disdain, the Ottomans appointed one of their Christian bureaucrats as governor of

Mount Lebanon. The next few years were filled with various political intrigues until January 1866 when Turkish forces attacked some of Karam's followers.

Sometime later, Karam and his men were being pursued by Ottoman infantry. As the chase was underway, the Turks passed through Zgharta. They pillaged the town. According to an account written by the Jesuit historian Joseph Goudard, the sanctuary of the Church of Our Lady "was devastated, the ancient painting sullied and burned on a pile of sacred ornaments, the [gold and silver] lamps torn out, and filth was strewn everywhere."[12] At the time Karam was in control of the nearby village of Benash'i but as the Turks approached it he and his men withdrew. Semaan Mkhayel Farchakh, who was positioned on high ground observing the advancing Ottomans, later told his children the land appeared to be a "sea of red ants," a reference to the red headdress worn by Turkish troops.[13] The Turks temporarily captured Benash'i and sacked the village but then, their advance faltered. When it did, Karam's men counterattacked under the command of Boutros Touma. The Turks were routed and in the process Touma and his men captured a number of weapons including cannons. The combination of cannon fire and Karam's forces, numbering about 800 men, caused the Ottoman lines to disintegrate. Under constant bombardment and assault, the retreating remnants of an estimated 5,000 Turkish soldiers were pushed all the way back to Tripoli.[14]

Karam and his followers planned to march on the Ottoman-appointed regime headquarters at Bayt al-Din, overthrow the governor and declare a self-ruled Christian Lebanon.[15] But, he was stopped in a battle east of Beirut with no allies to come to his aid. Nor would the European powers intervene on his behalf. Support for a national liberation movement in Lebanon was not part of the British or French imperialistic schemes.

The French counsel general in Beirut referred to Karam as a renegade, and Karam's quest for an independent Lebanon was termed a rebellion. Youssef Bey was forced into exile on the condition that his men were granted full amnesty.

He went to Algeria for a short time and then departed for Europe. He traveled across the continent lobbying governments to support his return to his homeland and the establishment of an independent Lebanon, but he was unsuccessful. He settled in Italy where he died in 1889. His un-embalmed body was brought back to Ehden and placed in a glass-top coffin in the church of Saint George. It can be viewed there today over a century after his death. To some, his uncorrupted body was proof of his saintliness and devotion to the Virgin Mary. He is revered by many as "the Liberator of Lebanon," one of the country's great national heroes.

The same year Youssef Karam went into exile, 1867, Semaan Mkhayel and Warda become parents for the first time. The baby girl was named Nazha but she did not survive childhood. She was followed by five siblings who all grew to adulthood. They were Sarkis (b.1870), Badawi, the Badawi Simon of this story (b.1873), Youssef (b.1876), a second daughter named Nazha (b.1881), and Rumanos (b.1885).[16]

Sarkis was named after a 4th century saint of the Armenian Apostolic Church. *Mar* (Saint) Sarkis was the most popular saint among the Syrian churches and numerous churches, convents and monasteries were named in his honor throughout Lebanon and Syria. The street in Ehden where an old monastery bears his name is Mar Sarkis Street. He is remembered as a knight-errant who rode a white charger and came to the aid of those who called to him in time of peril. He was also a Roman general but ended up being martyred for refusing to worship pagan gods. He was revered throughout the Byzantine Empire and continues to be remembered to this day among Eastern Churches including some in the US. Portrayals of Saint Sarkis often include Saint Bacchus who accompanied him on his rescue and military missions and met the same fate. In other languages, Sarkis is rendered as Santiago, Serge, Sergi, Sergio, Sergius, etc.

Badawi is a given name and sometimes a family name. Second only to Sarkis, it is the most prominent name among Farchakh men in North Lebanon. In all likelihood, Badawi Simon was named after his father's oldest brother, the first Farchakh to immigrate to the US and who later returned to Mount Lebanon. The origin of the name is somewhat obscure, but in its Christian usage, it is said to be a reference to Saint Anthony of Padua, or *Mar Antonius el Badwani*, in Arabic. Badawi also appears as a given and family name among non-Christians, so the reference to Saint Anthony would not apply. Possibly because there was no English equivalent to his given name, Badawi Simon sometimes abbreviated his given name with the initial "B." Around 1916, he replaced Badawi with the adopted name Bernard.

The name Youssef is the universal Joseph, Josef, Jose, Giuseppe, etc. and is not limited in usage to any particular religious, ethnic or social group. Until the naming of Semaan Mkhayel's third son, there were no other Farchakh men known as Youssef. It is possible that he was named in honor of Youssef Bey Karam.

Nazha, the name of the only daughter of Semaan Mkhayel and Warda who grew to adulthood, translates as "Gentle Lady." In the US, she was known as Rose or Rosa and, to the children of her brother Badawi Simon, she was *amte*, my father's sister.

Rumanos is the Greek version of the Latin name Romanus. For centuries it has been a popular given name in the Middle East. Historical figures named Rumanos include an early pope, a poet saint, and several emperors of the Byzantine Empire. In the US Rumanos Semaan Farchakh was known at different times as Rumanos Simon, Rumanos Simhan and Roman Simon. After his immigration to Brazil in the mid 1920s, he was known as Romao Simao, the Portuguese version of Roman Simon.

In the mid-1890s Sarkis married Latifi Mjelli, a blue-eyed blond of legendary beauty. So beautiful, according to old country lore, that she was instructed by none other than the Maronite Patriarch himself to dress in a long-sleeved garment that extended from her neck to her ankles whenever she appeared in public.[17] A year after their marriage, she gave birth to twin girls. In 1896 she had third child, a daughter named Najibi. The next year a son named Semaan was born. Of these children, only Najibi survived childhood. In 1898, Latifi gave birth to Boutros (Peter) Sarkis Farchakh who lived until 1985. His birth was followed by that of a brother named Boulos (Paul), and, a year later, Latifi gave birth to another son, Tannous (one of several versions of Anthony). It seemed that Sarkis and Latifi were on their way to having a large family, but not long after the birth of Tannous, tragedy struck. First, their oldest son, Semaan died. He was eight years old and had been blind for almost two years, the result of smallpox. Within a year, a more devastating tragedy occurred when Latifi and her newborn daughter both died from a fever. In addition to the grief over the loss of his wife and new baby, Sarkis was confronted with the need to provide a mother for his surviving children. Within a year of Latifi's death, he married Marin Mansour Sleiman from the village of Al Kattim. In 1907, they became parents to a son, appropriately named Semaan. Over the course of their marriage, Marin gave birth to seven children.[18]

Sarkis Semaan Farchakh 1893

A number of stories survive about Sarkis. The one most often recounted has to do with an event that occurred when he worked as a foreman in a silk mill near Zgharta. One of the social-liberating features of the silk industry in Mount Lebanon was its utilization of women workers who, up to the time of the silk factories, never worked outside the home.[19] The factory's machinery was driven by a combination of a coal-fired steam engine and waterwheel. For safety purposes women were required to keep their hair cut short or tied in a bun at the back of their heads. If their hair accidentally got caught in a loom, there was no way to quickly stop the machinery, and the woman would be injured or possibly killed before she could be freed. As the story goes, a young woman's long hair fell free and became caught in a loom. She was gradually being woven into the moving parts. Sarkis heard her scream and ran to investigate. Seeing that she was in grave peril, he shouted, "Sacred Heart, help me" and grabbed the main drive belt that powered the factory. There were 104 wheels driven by the main belt, and Sarkis stopped all of them. The skin on his forearms, hands and chest were severely skinned and burned, but the woman was cut loose.[20] Her life was saved and his feat immortalized. There is a curious similarity in this story regardless of whether one hears it in the US or in Lebanon. Family members thousands of miles apart who have never had any direct contact with each other tell the story the same way and the number of mill wheels Sarkis stopped is always 104.

Dynamics of Emigration

In the years before the Great War and for decades afterward, the indigenous population of what today is Lebanon was ethnically defined as Syrian. When Syrians and others from the Ottoman Empire emigrated, they usually traveled under Ottoman papers and were sometimes referred to as *Turcos*, that is, Turks. This Medieval Latin noun was used in several contexts, but to Lebanese and Syrian immigrants, especially in Central and South America, it was and continues to be an ancestral designation. The ethnic label Lebanese did not come into popular usage in the US until after World War II. Up until that time, those who were subsequently referred to as Lebanese were known as Syrians. The constitution for the State of Lebanon was adopted in 1926, but, four years later, when the 1930 US Census was taken, immigrants in the US originating from Mount Lebanon by and large continued to identify themselves as Syrian. In this story, the adjectives Syrian and Lebanese are often used interchangeably but are not intended to imply or suggest any particular political affiliation or affinity.

Throughout history, there have been movements of populations within Greater Syria, the Middle East and the world-at-large, but in the 19th century emigration from Lebanon became a remarkable phenomenon.

A trickle began in the aftermath of the 1860 Mount Lebanon civil war and continued for the next two decades. But in the early 1890s, it became a torrent when thousands of Lebanese men and women, married and single, immigrated to the west. The vast majority was Christian but not exclusively. Historian Albert Hourani writes that by 1914, when the Great War erupted, "about 300,000 Lebanese are said to have left."[1] Some mountain villages were virtually depopulated of its young people. The exodus was so pronounced in Mount Lebanon that the road leading out of Ehden to the lands below and the embarkation ports of Tripoli and Beirut became known as *The Way of the Emigrants*. There is no single cause of the emigration but rather a combination of intertwined factors that may be generally categorized under the broad headings of socio-economic and political.

During the 19th century, the people of Mount Lebanon lived in feudal society where they were categorized into two groups, *shaykh* and peasant. This dichotomy was a social designation, not necessarily an indicator of economic status. For example, a *shaykh* might have little tangible wealth, but he remained a *shaykh* while a peasant with substantial wealth remained a peasant. Each was confined to the social class into which he or she was born. The power of a *shaykh* was usually derived from his land holdings, control of silk manufacturing, influence with church leadership, other *shaykh* families, and loyalties based upon traditional interactions and kinship. Peasants generally fell into three groups: those who owned land and derived their livelihood from it, tenants who worked land owned by absentee owners, and semi-nomadic peasants. The latter group might work a piece of land for a year or two and then move their tent or temporary dwelling to another plot.[2]

By the middle of the 19th century, much of the wealth of Mount Lebanon was derived from the production of silk. Cultivable land was dominated by *toot shami*, the Damascus mulberry tree, on which silk worms fed. From the cocoons silk thread was obtained and woven into cloth. However, as the mid-19th century passed, silk crops became less and less productive. Adding to the woes of Mount Lebanon's silk-based economy was competition from the Far East. The price of silk originating in East Asia destined for European markets began to be sold at substantially lower prices as shipping costs decreased with the opening of the Suez Canal in 1869.[3]

During the years of prosperity and better living conditions, birth rates increased and the population of Mount Lebanon began to outgrow available resources. More sons meant that inherited land was parceled out in smaller plots often too small to provide the livelihood and relative degree of prosperity to which many in Mount Lebanon had become accustomed. Thus, the generation born after about 1860 began to look for alternate economic means beyond the boundaries of Syria.[4]

Some scholars writing in the latter part of the 20th century dismiss Lebanese grievances against Ottoman rule claiming that Christians were not persecuted by the Turks as purported. Among these scholars are some who challenge accounts that promulgate what they refer to as "the persecution myth."[5] Their view is based on the premise that those who wrote of Christian travails were writers and historians interested in gaining European sympathy for the establishment of an independent Lebanese state. This notion ignores other writers and historians who were not Turkish apologist but did not favor severing Lebanon from Syria. It also implicitly dismisses the realities of four centuries of militaristic Ottoman oppression, corruption, and stagnation. Regardless of the assumed political motivation by those who wrote about Ottoman excesses or whether the Turks were guilty of persecution or discrimination against Christians, other sources go beyond the limitation of semantics. Oral and written histories report that the Turks were not benevolent overlords who treated Christians and other religious groups with equanimity and tolerance.[6]

Policies originating in Istanbul, Constantinople of ancient and medieval history, capital of the Ottoman Empire, and enforced in the province of Syria alternated between severity and liberality. The degree of direct control versus some modicum of autonomy varied with the particular sultan and bureaucracy in power, but Ottoman policies became more oppressive during the autocratic reign of Abdul Hamid II. When he ascended to the Ottoman throne in 1876 the Arab world led by Syrian, Lebanese and Egyptian intellectuals (the latter often being Lebanese émigrés) was moving toward a revitalization of their cultural and Arabic linguistic heritages. At about the same time, the first stirrings of nationalism emerged.[7] The response from Constantinople to what Syrian historian George Antonius termed "the Arab awakening" was to centralize civil administration thus limiting local participation in governmental affairs. In addition to other "reforms," the Ottoman rulers were attempting to build political solidarity throughout their empire and, as part of this program, imposed the Turkish language on the Arabic-speaking population of Syria. This decree not only applied to legal and commercial matters but required Turkish to be the language of instruction in state schools.[8]

The Ottomans also employed the age-old imperial tactic of "divide and conquer," and, when practiced in Syria, it sometimes led to sectarian strife.[9] So-called reforms upset delicate sectarian balances and traditions, and, when the Turks played off one group against another and exploited old grievances, it sometimes led to civil chaos and bloodshed. The resulting loss of human life, damage to agriculture, livestock and property became the Ottoman justification for further intervention in

Syrian domestic affairs. It worked not only to sustain Constantinople's grip on Syria but also provided ostensible justification for military actions and political policies to the ever-watchful and territory-covetous European empires.[10]

Turkish rule sustained a feudal system under which some peasants lived on a level comparable to that of serfs. Ottoman policies were harsh and prejudicial against most everyone and laws were rigidly enforced. At times there were multiple and arbitrary taxes sometimes farmed out to corrupt tax collectors who extorted what they could from *shaykh* and peasant landowners alike and remitted to Constantinople the amount of money they thought the Ottoman treasury would deem satisfactory.[11]

There were times when the theocratic rulers in Constantinople could be fanatical. Their rigid interpretation of Islam led them to have limited tolerance for Christians because of certain beliefs and practices. There were times when prejudice led the Ottomans to require Christians to wear clothing that would distinguish them from Muslims. Disdain went beyond religious issues and into the political realm due to Ottoman suspicions that Christians harbored separatist ambitions or were part of a Fifth Column element working on behalf of European powers to undermine Turkish imperial interests. Turkish intolerance was not limited to Christians but extended to the Shia, Nusayri (also known as Alawite) and Mutawali Islamic sects, and members of the Druze faith. Each group was regarded in varying degrees as infidels, apostates, or heretics.

The level of intolerance and persecution visited upon these divergent confessional groups was mitigated on some occasions by the protection afforded them by France, Great Britain and Russia. Each empire used a method of expanding their imperial power in Ottoman-controlled lands by adopting the self-imposed task of protector of a religious group. The English looked after the Druze, the Russians took care of the Orthodox faiths, and the French were the protectors of the Maronites. Each imperial power sought privileges for their respective group that were often viewed by local elites as a zero-sum game in which their traditional status was threatened. Nineteenth century interference by the European powers in Syrian domestic matters was further exacerbated by Western missionaries who converted some local Christians to Protestantism. This created a religious community that had not previously existed and had an affect similar to Ottoman reforms because it too impinged upon fragile confessional arrangements and upset the status quo.[12]

In discussions about Nineteenth Century Lebanon there are occasions when two or more stories contain similarities or elements in common. With the passing of time bits and pieces are sometimes taken from each one and they become intertwined into a fictional rendering. One such example is the mixture of military conscription, irregular military service, the Ottoman policy of "boy tribute" and a later Ottoman policy of selecting talented youngsters for education in Istanbul.

Conscription had always been an incendiary undertaking in the Ottoman Empire's Arab provinces where young Muslim men were inducted almost always against their will to bolster Turkish forces. It usually meant being sent to a theatre of operations to fight Ottoman battles in far-flung lands over issues that meant nothing to Arab soldiers. Until the restoration of the 1876 Ottoman Constitution by the Young Turk movement in 1909, Christians were exempt from the draft. Nonetheless, serving in the Ottoman army had nothing to do with irregular military service where Lebanese and Syrian men were recruited or joined local militias to fight at the behest of their *shaykh* or chieftain. The men of Ehden and Zgharta who fought alongside Youssef

Bey Karam are one such example. But this sort of irregular military service was typically not far from home and of limited duration. It was not comparable to the years of service and absence away from family that was required by the Ottoman army which could be economically devastating to farmers and family breadwinners.

Another form of military service utilized by the Ottoman government was the "boy tribute." According to historian Roderick H. Davison, "a system of levying a tribute of boys from Christian subjects was organized... [under which]...boys in their teens or younger were taken from Christian families, screened, tested, trained in various schools [in Constantinople], and then enrolled in the Janissary corps," an elite military unit of the Ottoman army.[13] Although this practice was generally limited to Albania and the Balkan states and abandoned in 1826, it is recounted because it lingered as part of immigrant lore sometimes used to explain why male ancestors migrated from Greater Syria. However, there is no evidence that the "boy tribute" was ever extended east or south of Anatolia, the land mass on which Turkey is located. Confusing the boy tribute with events that occurred during the early Twentieth Century reign of Abdul Hamid II also led to fictional stories. Under this particular Ottoman program academically talented Syrian boys were selected for advanced education and sent to Istanbul for schooling. This practice had nothing to do with military service and was usually in preparation for work in government bureaucracies.[14]

The Immigrant Experience and the Simon's First Emigration

Regular steamship routes in and around the Mediterranean were established and in use by the middle of the 19th century. Steamship agents traveled to towns and villages throughout Mount Lebanon promoting their service and making the availability of passenger tickets easy. Although passage from Lebanon to the Americas cost ten to fifteen dollars, it was a substantial amount of money at the time especially for the peasant class. Immigrants often funded their trip by selling personal possessions or borrowing money from friends, relatives, or money-lenders.[1]

There were times when immigrants left their spouse and children with relatives in the old country and sent for them later when they were established in their new countries and could afford to purchase more tickets. Once an individual or community was established in a new land, family members and others from the old country village or town would emigrate and join them.[2] Sometimes it took years to get all the members of a family from the old country to the new homeland. One such example occurred when Kahlil and Zakia Zoghby emigrated from Mount Lebanon to Mobile, Alabama in 1901. Because they did not have sufficient funds to buy tickets for their family all at one time, they had their children sent from the old country in three intervals. The last one arrived in the US in 1910, and the family was finally reunited after being separated for nine years.[3]

A voyage from Beirut to a European port was a comparatively easy trip. Once in the French ports of Marseille or Le Havre, emigrants destined for New York and other US ports boarded an ocean liner for crossing the Atlantic. This leg of the trip was quite different than the first one. Early immigrants more often than not booked passage at the lowest fare which meant "Third Class" or steerage.[4] Voyages were uncomfortable and unhealthy and not without the loss of life. When the ocean liner *Titanic* collided with an iceberg in the North Atlantic and sank in 1912 there were 154 Syrian emigrants aboard. Some of them were from Zgharta. Twenty-nine Syrians were saved, 125 perished.[5]

Few ships met the fate of the *Titanic,* but many were dirty and overcrowded and oftentimes men, women and children who had never traveled over water became seasick. Food was meager. As the eighteen-day crossing ended and Ellis Island was in sight, anxiety increased with the possibility of being refused entry because of some real or imagined reason, usually medically related. Those rejected never entered the US but were sent back to their ship and crossed the Atlantic again. There were instances when immigrants returned to Le Havre or Marseille and had no money to buy a ticket to their homeland. Sometimes they remained stranded for weeks, months and in some cases, years.[6]

There were reasons beyond being turned back at Ellis Island for immigrants to cross the Atlantic more than once. Often, it was a matter of choice and was not an isolated or unusual occurrence. A historian of the Arab immigrant experience, Alexa Naff, writes that the first wave of Syrian immigrants did not intend to make their permanent homes in the Americas. Their migration was a conscious and temporary venture intended to improve their economic status. In the US, most of them, men and women, turned to peddling which was strenuous and sometimes dangerous, but, once the desired amount of money was accumulated, they returned home. With newly acquired wealth, some built homes, often with red tile roofs which became the hallmark of a returning immigrant.[7] Those who returned to Mount Lebanon sometimes remained there while others traveled back to the US to earn additional money and bring relatives and friends. According to some estimates, at least forty percent of pre-World War One Syrian immigrants returned home after meeting their economic goals or for other reasons.[8] There were also cases where immigrants traveled to the west, didn't like what they found or were unable to adjust to life away from the traditionalism of Lebanon and returned home, but immigrant studies indicate they were a relatively small number.

The immigration phenomenon became ingrained in Lebanese culture to such an extent that, decades later, grandchildren of the original 19th century immigrants who visited Lebanon for the first time were themselves referred to as immigrants. Manifestations of immigrant culture are found in many venues throughout contemporary Lebanon including university emigration research departments, national histories, family stories, and even certain jokes. In the arts, a perennially popular story portraying events in the life of an immigrant returning to homeland after living in Australia for several decades is George Shehade's, *The Emigrant of Brisbane.*

In the spring of 1890, Badawi, Catherine, and Sarkis along with other emigrants boarded a ship in Tripoli for the two-thousand mile voyage to Marseille. They made ports of call at several Mediterranean harbors including Larnaca, Cyprus and Genoa, Italy.[9] If their destination had been New York or another US eastern port, they would have boarded a train to take them from Marseilles to Paris and onto the Channel Port of Le Havre on the Normandy coast. For destinations other than the east coast of the US, as in the case of the Simons, they would board a ship bound for Havana, Cuba. During those years, Havana served as a hub for passengers traveling west from European ports. Once in Havana, they disembarked. Emigrants might remain in Cuba, but more often than not they boarded one of the ships that fanned out across the Caribbean. They steamed to a number of ports in Central and South America and destinations on the southern US coast such as Mobile and New Orleans.[10]

Once they had arrived in Havana, Badawi, Catherine, and Sarkis boarded a ship bound for the Yucatan Peninsula. There they disembarked at the port of Progresso and traveled to Merida, the capital of Yucatan. Almost a decade before the first wave of Lebanese immigrants came to the US, Mexico had become a preferred destination. The first recorded Lebanese to land in Mexico was Father Boutros Raffoul in 1878. He was followed the next year by Santiago Souma, considered the founder of the Lebanese community in Yucatan. A large migration continued for several decades and among the early families who established themselves were several from Zgharta.[11] No doubt the Simons had friends and relatives living there.[12] Whether they traveled to Yucatan to visit friends and relatives or investigate the possibility of settling there is not known, but is it safe to conclude they brought letters and news from Mount Lebanon.

The Simons remained in Yucatan for several weeks. In May 1890, they returned to Progresso and boarded a ship bound for New Orleans. At the time, there was a small Syrian community there including some from Zgharta. One such man was Boutros Yammine who arrived in the US in 1885. In later years more emigrants from Zgharta came to New Orleans and Mobile.[13]

If the Simons or any other immigrants coming to the US in the second half of the 19[th]century imagined they would be universally welcomed with open arms, they were sorely mistaken. This was not a phenomenon unique to the US, but in some ways it was more pronounced. One of the characteristics of nation-states is homogeneity; that is, the population has some sort of cohesive group feeling that binds them together in the form of a national identity. It might be ethnicity, religion, language, or a combination of these and other elements. That was less true for the US because it was a nation of immigrants in which each group had its own cultural, religious and linguistic heritage. This reality did not prevent differing ideas from gaining acceptance such as the special identity of the country's founders, the reasons for its establishment, and justification for its existence.

Like other nation-states, the US developed its own set of national myths. Among those cherished in the pre-Civil War era was the belief that the early settler population was a special group destined to fulfill some grand plan for mankind. The myth included the notion that the American "race" was a homogeneous body that enjoyed the special attention of God.[14] That this special people had white skin was a tacitly understood fact. These mythical concepts were eloquently expressed a few years after the US gained its independence by John Jay in 1787 when he wrote in Federalist Paper Number 2 "that Providence has been pleased to give this one connected country to one united people---a people descended from the same ancestors, speaking the same language, professing the same religion, attached to the same principles of government [and] very similar in their manners and customs."[15] His delineation of the characteristics of "one united people" sounds like a description of the English speaking Protestant colonists, but it clearly did not include Native Americans who were thought of as savages or African slaves, the chattel of an agrarian economic system. In other words, Jay's assumptions were part of the national myth. The "one united people" notion was fairly safe until after the Civil War when it was challenged by the second wave of immigrants who came to the US. Until that time, the American population seems to have viewed itself as being largely the descendents of the first wave trail blazers and founding settlers from northwestern Europe: England, Ireland, Germany and the Scandinavian countries.

In contrast to this premise, many immigrants that comprised the post-Civil War wave were not from those countries that traditionally added to the US population and, as a result, were received in different ways depending upon the geographical area where they settled and who their advocates and adversaries were.[16] For example, as industrialization began to expand, immigrants were seen as a source of cheap labor and potential customers for consumer goods manufactured in the factories of a robust and growing economy. As a source of cheap labor, business owners and related interest groups opposed any government attempt to enact immigration regulating legislation. While cheap labor might have added to the profits of business owners it also led to conflict between American "native stock" wage earners who lost their jobs to immigrants who were desperate for work and willing to take jobs for less money.[17]

In an atmosphere of considerable debate, beginning in the 1880s Congress enacted legislation to lessen worker tensions between "old Americans" and "new Americans" and establish the foundations for federal restriction of immigration. Contract labor law was expanded to deny admission to immigrants answering potential employers' want ads that ran in their home country newspapers, ads that in-and-of-themselves Congress had declared illegal. Other laws passed at that time included the first workable means for deporting aliens residing in the US including those who had entered illegally or gone onto state welfare rolls. Earlier legislation was expanded to bar admission of polygamists and "persons suffering from a loathsome or dangerous contagious disease."[18]

Legislation passed by Congress was only one aspect of the immigrant controversy. Other ideas surfaced and some predicted dire consequences for the country as a result of the second immigrant wave. One such prediction was the result of a study conducted by Francis A. Walker, president of Massachusetts Institute of Technology. It was based on his interpretation of the reasons for the declining rate of population growth among America's "native stock." While many observers noted that the decrease was probably linked to urbanization and industrialization, Walker came to the conclusion that native-stock Americans were having fewer children because they preferred to maintain their standard of living rather than have large families. Their standard of living, he continued, was being threatened because immigrants underbid them in the workplace and out-bred them at home. His conclusion was that native-stock Americans were being replaced by immigrants. On the other hand, contrary facts hardly supported his contentions. Until 1896, immigrants from northern and western Europe surpassed in number those of less desirable origin such as southern and eastern Europe. Writing in 1955 historian John Higham stated that "at least eighty percent of the European-born population of the United States in the mid-nineties [1890s] still derived from…Germany, Great Britain, Scandinavia, France, Switzerland, and the Low Countries."[19]

Many immigrants settled in the large cities of the East and Midwest. The loudest anti-immigrant sentiments were found among nativist Americans in the north and northeast. Varying economic conditions caused nativism and racism to raise its heads especially during times of economic downturn or depression. When this happened, violent incidents were often part of labor disputes. As the number of immigrant workers, largely German, Irish and Italian, entered the work force in northern factories and other places like the iron and coal mines around Birmingham, Alabama, they unionized. Labor unrest was blamed on German anarchists while in the arena of big city politics, the Irish were seen as the source of corruption in municipal governments particularly in New York and Boston. Added to the economic and labor factors was a strong anti-Catholic movement that painted Catholic immigrants, especially Irish and Italians, as agents of the Pope who intended to overthrow the American republic by armed insurrection and place the country under papal control.[20]

In various parts of the US, it was difficult if not impossible in some cases for immigrants to find work in certain fields, especially those who were non-declarant aliens, that is, immigrants who had not declared their intention of becoming naturalized Americans. For example, certain states outlawed immigrants from taking white collar jobs; some required attorneys to be American citizens, and, in 1909, the State of New York prohibited immigrants from being private detectives. In Michigan, an alien could not get a barber's license. But in the South things were different. Shifting demographics and the associated economic effects created a demand for workers. Some states seized the offensive to reduce their labor shortages, and, from 1903 until 1907, seven southern states created or reactivated immigration bureaus to entice immigrants to come to their state. Some initiated elaborate plans such as one in South

Carolina that went so far as to pay the passenger fees for a shipload of Belgian textile workers. When they arrived in Charleston, they were greeted by a cheering crowd, provided a free lunch and extended an official welcome.[21]

In the years between the turn of the century and the outbreak of The Great War in 1914, immigrants from numerous countries poured into the US. In Mount Lebanon, "American fever" grew ever larger as Syrian emigration continued. Often times, their first stop was New York City and just as often they were advised to "go south." [22] This was not necessarily an attempt to encourage them to move on but a practical suggestion in light of the growing industrial development of the south. Many of the first-wave newcomers heeded this advice and moved to the land of Dixie where they successfully established businesses in Alabama, Mississippi and Louisiana.

One of the industries in the South that was undergoing continuing expansion was the railroads. They, along with cotton farmers and cotton mills, were confronted with major labor shortages as southerners migrated from the south faster than outsiders could arrive. This was particularly true for African-Americans who gravitated from rural areas to nearby towns and cities. From there, many thousands moved to cities in the north. As migrations of the Southern population continued, immigrants were seen as a solution to the growing labor shortage. For some the arrival of immigrants was viewed as a means of accelerating the African-American exodus from the south.[23]

In this complex and sometimes hostile environment, immigrants competed for jobs that were often performed under less than desirable or unsafe working conditions, often at exploitative wages. Stories abound of their experiences in the industrial, mining, meat-packing, and other industries. Generally speaking, Syrians did not seek jobs in the industrialized workplace as did other immigrant groups. Working for someone other than themselves was not viewed as a path to prosperity nor was it comparatively lucrative. In terms of personal income, peddlers earned more dollars per day of work than did factory laborers.[24] For this and other reasons, Badawi Simon and his brother Sarkis followed the course chosen by an estimated ninety-percent of pre-Great War Syrian immigrants. They became peddlers.[25]

In the style of other Syrian peddlers, the Simon brothers were supplied merchandise by a peddler outfitter, an independent businessman, usually Syrian, who had been in the US for several years. It was in the outfitter's commercial interest to have a steady stream of immigrants arriving from the old country to expand his sales force, and in this role he often furnished tickets for passage to fellow villagers, relatives or acquaintances. He acted as sponsor and adviser to new arrivals and set them up to peddle merchandise. He supplied them with goods on credit and showed them which routes to work. It was not unusual for peddlers to give their money to their outfitter for safe keeping. Because of the economic interdependence of the outfitter-peddler relationship, there was little exploitation and dissatisfaction.[26]

Although the term "peddler" might invoke images somewhat pejorative in our "post-modern" 21st century, that was not the case in the turn-of-the-century rural South. In the 1890s, there were no malls, shopping centers, factory outlet stores, or retail discount chains. The route peddler performed an essential service to rural customers by offering an assortment of goods for sale or barter and delivering special items ordered on earlier sales calls. People living in rural areas did not travel to towns and cities very often, so having clothing, house wares and other goods brought to their front door was a welcome service. A social feature of the peddler-consumer relationship was the news and gossip he or she brought along and discussed over an evening meal. This was a common occurrence when an itinerant salesperson bartered some of his or her wares for supper and a place to sleep. Writing in 1924 about early Syrian peddlers, historian Philip Hitti noted that they were "the connecting link between the lace or white goods merchant and the consumer, generally the housewife." [27]

Badawi and Sarkis were assigned a route that took them into the rural Mississippi River delta of Louisiana. The merchandise they initially peddled was notions and soft goods. This was an inordinately strenuous way to earn a living. A route peddler who could not afford a horse and carriage or a cart usually packed merchandise into a suitcase-type container that was strapped to his back. When fully loaded, it could weigh well over one hundred pounds. In each hand he might carry a notions case containing pins, needles, sewing thread, combs, scissors, and other items. For the more vigorous peddler, there might be an additional container that hung over his chest. Years after Badawi Simon's peddler days had ended, Catherine told stories about working the sales routes with him. She said the work was strenuous to such a degree that on more than one occasion she saw him spit up blood.[28]

Working all day in the Mississippi Delta of Louisiana posed risks ranging from over-exposure to the elements to being robbed or falling victim to a natural disaster. In one episode, the two Simon brothers traveled to a rural area to collect money they were owed. Without warning, river waters began to rise, and they were caught in a flash flood. Neither one could swim, but Badawi was rescued by a man in a small boat. Sarkis was in water literally over his head but he managed to survive by bobbing up and down. When he sank he would spring off the bottom and break through the surface to get air before going under again. He was convinced he was going to drown, but he too was finally rescued.[29]

After their time in New Orleans, Badawi, Catherine, and Sarkis traveled to Mobile, Alabama where the two brothers continued to work as route peddlers. Writing to his father in March 1892, Badawi acknowledged receipt of his January 4 letter. Badawi went on to explain that he planned to remain in the US for one year which would have been until about March 1893. He included greetings to his father from other Zghartawis living in Mobile and New Orleans at the time: Boutros Rumanos Yammine, Barbar Badawi Namy, Sarkis Youssef Tatin, Assad Antoine Jabbour, and Boutros el Khoury, a cousin of Catherine's subsequently known in the US as Pete Khoury.[30] Although there was a functioning postal system within the domain of the Ottoman Empire, letters between correspondents in the US and Mount Lebanon were usually carried by relatives and other travelers. In addition to providing news from the US, letters often included money for family members to pay mortgages, buy land, or pay other expenses. In early 1893 it was time to prepare for the return to Lebanon via Mexico as Badawi had told his father the previous year, but, by this time, Catherine learned she was pregnant. It was decided that Sarkis would travel ahead to Mexico where Badawi and Catherine would join him after the birth of their baby.[31]

According to entries Badawi Simon made on a blank page in his Bible, he and Catherine were parents to eight children. Their first child was a son named Aziz, a traditional Arabic name meaning "dear." His baptismal name was Semaan (Simon). He was born May 17, 1893 in New Orleans. Because the Farchakh surname was not used by his father, Aziz's American name was Aziz Badawi Simon. Sometime between 1910 and 1916, he adopted the name Farshee which is the contemporary US family's name. The name Farshee is not unique to the US Simon family and is found among a few other American families not related to the Simons, Farchakhs, or their descendants. Within the US family and the old Syrian community in Alabama, the first Simon son was known as Aziz but the name he used as an adult was Sim or Simon B. Farshee. He was also known as "Doc" after he took a job in 1903 as a delivery boy for a Mobile, Alabama druggist.[32]

Toward the end of 1893, Badawi, Catherine, and Aziz were ready to make the postponed trip to Mexico and link up with Sarkis. They boarded a ship in New Orleans and journeyed to Saint Petersburg, Florida. The cost of tickets for the three travelers totaled ten dollars. Once in Saint Petersburg, Badawi found himself broke. He wrote to Sarkis addressing the letter to Santiago Simon, the Spanish equivalent of Sarkis Semaan who was working in Merida awaiting the arrival of his brother and sister-in-law and their new-born son.[33]

In his letter to Sarkis, Badawi extended greeting to certain individuals by non-specific kinship names, not personal names and are therefore not identifiable. But Badawi never got to Mexico. In the letter he explained to Sarkis that he had loaned fifty dollars to his "dear cousin," Assad Leon. When Badawi asked Assad for repayment, the money was not available. No surviving letters reveal the degree of discouragement Badawi expressed in his 1893 letter when he wrote, "Honest to God and to you we do not have any money in our account or otherwise we would have returned [with you] from our immigration."[34] Without money for traveling, Badawi and Catherine could not bring their immigration to an end as planned and remained in the US for four more years. In late 1893, after several months in Mexico, Sarkis returned to Lebanon by way of Havana and Marseille. The two brothers did not see each other again until the summer of 1897.

Badawi and his little family remained in Tampa–Saint Petersburg while he turned again to peddling in an effort to improve their economic situation. He worked six days a week for several months. In the course of his business dealings, he learned from an acquaintance that a grocery store in Jacksonville would soon be available for rent. Perceiving what he thought to be a good business opportunity, he and Catherine traveled there in early 1894 to see for themselves what the opportunity might have in store for them. They determined that the terms of the lease were reasonable and the location, the corner of what are now First and Main streets, was good. By spring 1894 they had relocated to Jacksonville, signed the lease, and were on their way to recovering from the economic setbacks of the previous year.[35] They became acquainted with the few Syrians who lived there, including George Eid Ljhawi from Beirut and a woman identified as the mother of Shikri Hinini. When the Simon's second child Mary was born in July 1894, these two fellow Syrians served as godparents for her baptism at the Immaculate Conception church.[36] Like her older brother and later siblings, she was given a traditional name, Azizi, the feminine form of Aziz. Her baptismal name was Mary. Her full name was Mary Badawi Simon. Twenty years later when she married a Syrian immigrant, Zaki Azar, she was listed in the marriage records of Saint Peter's Catholic Church in Montgomery, Alabama as Mary B. Simon.

Badawi devoted certain days of the week to route peddling and on others worked in the store with Catherine. Because it was a neighborhood store, credit was extended to regular customers but the most desirable clientele were those who paid cash for their purchases. Catherine worked in the store and proved to be an astute businesswoman and salesperson. An anecdotal story from this period occurred one day when both Badawi and Catherine were in the store. Catherine was explaining to a lady customer the intricacies of a doily, *phutah* in Arabic, which she had made. A man walked in and approached Badawi. Greetings were exchanged, and the man asked Badawi for a pound of fresh salt meat. In reply, Badawi began to explain that he sold salt meat but salting was a preserving process and there was no such thing as "fresh" salt meat. Catherine, talking and listening at the same time, turned from her customer and told Badawi that a "fresh" supply had arrived the previous day when he was out. She proceeded to the meat counter and removed the bottom slab. She showed it to the man and told him it was fresh. He took it, paid Badawi, and departed. Catherine returned to her lady customer who bought the doily. After both customers were gone, she explained to Badawi that he should never let a potentially cash paying customer leave the store without selling him or her something.[37]

The US economy was in the midst of a brutal depression from 1893 to 1897, but the hard-working young couple prevailed. The grocery store and peddling businesses were monetarily rewarding, and the Simons did well during their Jacksonville years. In early summer 1897, they decided it was time to return to Mount Lebanon. They sold their interest in the store along with Badawi's peddler paraphernalia and, with the proceeds and accumulated savings, departed for Lebanon.[38] The immigration that was to continue for one year according to what Badawi had written to his father in 1892 came to an end five years later. During those years, the Simons had learned how to successfully operate a neighborhood grocery store as well as the ins and outs of route peddling. Reportedly, they carried a sizeable sum of money with them back to Lebanon.[39]

They departed the US in July 1897. Crossing the Atlantic Ocean was about an eighteen day trip but traveling from a southern US port to Havana added a few days. To carry her two toddlers, Catherine improvised a cloth sling which she hung around her neck. In one side she carried Aziz, in the other side, Mary.[40] Whatever discomfort she might have endured traveling by train or aboard ships in hot and humid conditions was heightened by the fact she was seven months pregnant when they left Jacksonville. The Simons did not travel directly from the US to Marseille but disembarked at La Havre on the Normandy coast and boarded the train to Paris. This was the usual way immigrants and others traveled between the northern Channel port of Le Havre and the Mediterranean port of Marseille. After a shopping and sightseeing spree of several days in Paris, they proceeded by train to Marseille.[41] From there, they steamed eastward for about a week with a few ports of call en route to Tripoli, North Lebanon. The trip from the US to Lebanon, from beginning to end, lasted thirty days.

At the time the Simons arrived to Lebanon, it was summertime, and Badawi's parents and most of the population of Zgharta were living in their summer homes in Ehden. The return of an immigrant son and his family was a highly joyous and festive event. Lebanese are openly affectionate within their family, and the Simons would have been repeatedly kissed and hugged. Their first greeting from relatives and friends probably included a loud *zalaglit*, the high-pitched trill Arabs make in times of grief or happiness. Coffee and sweets would have been served in every home they visited, and numerous celebrations would have welcomed the emigrants home. Gifts filled a trunk the Simons brought from Paris that were distributed to friends and relatives, a long-standing tradition still practiced today when travelers return home from a journey.

It was the first time Semaan Mkhayel and Warda had seen their oldest grandchildren, Aziz, 4 and Mary, 3, but more good news was in store. On September 13, Catherine gave birth to her third child, a son named Jamil, "beautiful" in Arabic. He was given the baptismal name, Mema, the same name as the first Maronite church built in Ehden.[42] However, in the US he used his traditional name sparingly and at no time his baptismal name. Instead, he was known by his adopted name, John (John in Arabic is *Hanna* and is not a translation of Jamil). Consequently, in his youth and young adult years, he was known as John B. Simon and served in the US Army during World War I under that name. Later he changed his surname to Farshee and established himself as John B. Farshee. But, within the immediate and extended family and to friends, he was known as Johnny.

Nonetheless, having all their family at home proved to be a short-lived joy for Semaan Mkhayel and Warda as the lure of "American fever," as immigration was called, persisted. In 1898 Badawi's seventeen year-old sister, Nazha, married their first cousin, Mansour Leon, a son of Jabbour Lawon Karam and Samira Zedda. Shortly after their marriage, the young couple immigrated to the US making their home in Mobile.[43]

Sometime in 1898, Badawi began to talk of returning to the US. He had mentioned that he wanted to go back to Mobile with Mansour and Nazha. Whether he had originally intended to return to the US after a visit of several months in Lebanon or whether he came to realize he could not readjust to living there after living in the US is not known for certain. Neither of these scenarios was unique. Many returning immigrants often went through the same processes. They would return to the old country with money, sometimes buy land or build a home only to discover they could not make a social transition in reverse. There is no hard documentation to confirm Badawi's intention to visit Lebanon and return to the US, but there are indications that when he went back to the old country it was for a visit, not to remain there.[44]

At the time, Semaan Mkhayel was close to sixty years old, and his wife Warda was near fifty. Hoping to spend their remaining years or perhaps at least a few of them surrounded by their family was to them a reasonable expectation. But there was another factor that fed their anxieties over Badawi's emigration. In the 1890s, there was no such thing as retirement programs or social security in Mount Lebanon. Homes for the aged were out of the question. When a parent became ill or too old to work, their wellbeing became the responsibility of the sons. There was no other way for old people to be provided for. In the case of Semaan Mkhayel and Warda, they were beginning to see the gradual disintegration of their family through emigration. It is true that many emigrants traveled abroad and eventually returned home to live permanently, but Semaan Mkhayel and Warda's fear was that their children would emigrate and they would never see them again.

Badawi's continuous talk of returning to the US was unnerving to his parents, and Semaan Mkhayel was adamant in his opposition to the idea. Undaunted by his parents' objections, Badawi persisted in pressing the issue. Opportunity in the US, he argued, with all its associated problems, hard work and disappointments was better than living in Mount Lebanon where there were few opportunities for ambitious young men. Some of his motives to emigrate were altruistic. Not only would he be able to send funds to his parents, he hoped to accumulate sufficient money to eventually build an orphanage which he expressed as one of his life's goals.[45]

By nature he was not an argumentative person, but when he made up his mind to do something, he could be very stubborn. Finally, Semaan's patience with his son's insistence reached its limit, and tempers exploded between the obstinate father and stubborn son. The disagreement became so heated that at one point Semaan Mkhayel told Badawi to go ahead and return to the US but leave Catherine and the children with him and Warda in Zgharta. If Badawi agreed to this condition, it would have been Semaan Mkhayel's assurance that his son would eventually return home, but this proposition was out of the question for Badawi or Catherine. Whether Semaan's outburst about Catherine and the children remaining in Zgharta was his and Warda's idea or an indication of their sympathy with Catherine's wishes is not clear. It might have been both. Details of what occurred after the flash of tempers are not recorded, but time passed, attitudes cooled, and a potential domestic crisis was averted. Semaan Mkhayel and Warda agreed to their son's wish to emigrate on the condition that he, Catherine, and the children remain in Lebanon for another year.[46]

When the year was up, Semaan Mkhayel provided his son with sufficient money in gold coin for emigrating.[47] Much of the money Badawi had when he returned to Mount Lebanon went toward the purchase of land. In 1899, after about two years in the old country, Badawi, Catherine, and their three children left Zgharta. They traveled to Tripoli where they boarded a ship and steamed from Lebanon to France and on to the US. Over time, the fear harbored by Semaan Mkhayel and Warda about the disintegration of their family through emigration was confirmed. Nazha, their only daughter who emigrated in 1898, never returned to Mount Lebanon nor did Badawi and Catherine and their children. Rumanos, the youngest son, immigrated to Mobile in 1903 and in early 1905 the third Farchakh brother, Youssef, married Adlah Kamfousch, and the couple immigrated to Brazil. Sometime before the outbreak of the Great War, Youssef and Adlah and their three children returned to Lebanon for a visit, but by that time Semaan Mkhayel had died.

A New Home in America: Mobile

In its colorful and sometimes turbulent history, Mobile, Alabama, has been at one time or another under the flags of France, Great Britain, and Spain. Being part of a European empire came to an end in 1813 when it was taken from Spain by the US Army. It was annexed by the US and, four years, later incorporated into the Alabama territory. The next year, 1818, Alabama joined the Union.[1]

Like other ports along the Gulf Coast, Mobile had seen good times and bad times. Good times abounded in pre-Civil War years when its deep water harbor served as a major embarkation port for the export of cotton; bad times during Yellow Fever epidemics, the 1864 bombardment and blockade during the Civil War by the Union Navy and municipal bankruptcy in 1879. In the decades following the Civil War, the bad times persisted; Mobile languished under Reconstruction and the general economic deterioration that plagued the South. Political corruption was rampant, the export of cotton disrupted, and the banking industry was unstable, all having detrimental effects on commerce. Then, around the turn of the century, Mobile's economic recovery started as the city began to industrialize.[2] Like other growing towns and cities in the industrialization process, Mobile was a magnet to Syrian peddlers and other immigrants. An expanding economy meant jobs for a growing population, and the related payrolls provided people with money to spend.

At the turn of the 19th and 20th centuries, Mobile's center of activity was in the downtown vicinity on and around Government Street. This boulevard, a century old at the time the Simons arrived there, was lined with old oak trees, government offices, commercial establishments, antebellum homes, and newer private residences. One of those houses, located at 58 Government Street, was rented by a Syrian immigrant named Fatah Bowab who came to the US in 1895. It was a large house, and, in those days, it was not unusual for home dwellers to rent out spare rooms to help defray expenses and provide supplemental income. That's what Fatah Bowab did. He had several lodgers, and among them were Badawi Simon and his family.[3]

The Simons and their landlord were not the only Syrians living in Mobile in 1899. There were Syrian lodgers at 58 Government Street including Khalil Seleus, Joseph Abod and Mary Khuri and her eighteen-year-old son, George.[4] Hanna Boutros Yammine, whose father Boutros Yammine was Aziz's godfather, were among friends and relatives from Ehden and Zgharta living in Mobile. Hanna Boutros arrived in Mobile with the Simons in 1899, the others around the same time. A few of the Mobile Syrians were grocers, but most were peddlers. A smaller number operated stores such as Badawi's friend Kabul Zahra who owned a dry goods store near the corner of 8th and Main Streets.[5] Nazha and Mansour Leon, Badawi's sister and brother-in-law, had worked as route peddlers when they first came to the US but later operated a grocery store where they lived in the second floor apartment. Other Simon relatives living in and around Mobile included Pete Khoury, Catherine Simon's cousin, who was a professional gambler.[6] Also living in Mobile were Badawi's first cousins, Mansour Leon's brother Assad and Assad's wife Saydeh.[7]

Another newcomer who settled in Mobile around the turn of the century was Faris Azar Salloum Hawie. He left his home village of Shuweir (variously spelled) in Mount Lebanon in 1895 when he was fifteen years old. His emigration, it was said, was made to avoid military conscription but that is an improbable contention considering he was Greek Orthodox, and Christians were not drafted into the Ottoman army until 1909. He first settled in the New York City area with his brother Alec and their cousin Michael. With money brought from the old country, the Hawies opened a factory manufacturing religious articles that were sold by Syrian peddlers and others.[8] Rosaries, statues of holy persons, wood carvings with religious motifs, Bibles, and other articles of devotion were popular items for Syrian peddlers to sell. Sometimes they promoted their religious wares as products from the Holy Land which was an honest contention providing their goods came from Lebanon or Palestine. During the lifetime of Jesus of Nazareth and for centuries afterward, Palestine—like Lebanon—was an integral part of Greater Syria. Furthermore, the travels of Jesus were not limited to Palestine. The Gospel of Matthew tells that he journeyed to Tyre on Lebanon's southern coast. Further confirmation that the Holy Land extended into Lebanon is based on a particular belief held by Lebanese and Syrian Christians and Muslims. Many of them believe that the wedding feast of Cana recorded in the Gospel of John occurred in the South Lebanon village of the same name but spelled Qana. According to Scripture, Jesus attended a wedding feast there and performed his first miracle.

As for the fate of the Hawie enterprise and the manufacture of religious items, the economy was in depression and competition stiff. After about two years, the venture failed. Alec and Michael went their separate ways, and Faris relocated to Mobile. He established himself as a dry goods merchant and, at the same time, became a peddler outfitter.[9] Badawi Simon had learned the ins and outs of route peddling during his first immigration and did not require Faris's guidance. But he did need sources of supply for the goods he peddled, and this led him to have commercial dealings with his fellow Syrian. Even if they had shared no commercial interests, they would have known each other because the Syrian community was close knit in those days, and, in Mobile, most of them lived within close proximity to each other in the downtown area.

By 1901, in addition to Badawi's peddler business, he and Catherine were operating a grocery store on Royal Street a few blocks from the historic antebellum Battle House Hotel. They had moved from Fatah Bouab's boarding house into their own living quarters behind the store. Things were going well for the Simons. They were operating an ongoing business, and, in July, their third son, Said (Sy Forshee), was born.[10]

His birth was a festive occasion, and, after the baptismal ceremony at the Cathedral of the Immaculate Conception on nearby Claiborne Street,[11] friends and relatives joined the baby boy's godparents, Hanna Boutros Yammine and Nazha, at the Simon home.[12] Guests brought traditional Lebanese foods such as tabbuli, mjadra, lebna, kibbi and sweets. The meal was followed by *mughli,* a rice-based pudding served during the celebration of a baby's birth. The ever-present symbol of hospitality and cordiality, *qahwi,* Arabic coffee, was served sweeter than usual because it was a happy occasion. Badawi's friend Kabul Zahra offered the congratulatory toast. The next year, in October 1902, Sy's baby sister was born. She was named Jamileh, the feminine form of

Jamil. The Simons' friend and former landlord Fatah Bowab was her godfather, Nazha her godmother.[13]

Beginning in his early years, young Aziz worked in the family grocery store and sometimes traveled with his father. Two years after Sy's birth, 1903, when Aziz was ten years old, he took a job as a delivery boy for Ortman Brothers Drug Company. It was this job that led Aziz to acquire the moniker Doc.[14] The nickname stuck. It became even more appropriate in his late teen and early adult years when he worked first as a druggist in Montgomery, Alabama and in the following decade after his formal education as an optometrist.

One of the reasons Aziz went to work at Ortman's was because his help was no longer needed in the grocery store. In 1903, more than six hundred thousand immigrants came to the US and among them was Badawi Simon's youngest brother, Rumanos Semaan Farchakh. His parents, Semaan Mkhayel and Warda, must have continued to believe that their sons would eventually return to Mount Lebanon or they would not have provided money for Rumanos's emigration. He was eighteen years old and at the time not sufficiently proficient in spoken English. It was decided that he should work in the Simons' grocery store until his language skills improved. In his new role, Rumanos worked with Catherine which freed up Badawi to spend more time working his peddler route.[15] Some of the time Rumanos worked with his sister Nazha and her husband Mansour in their grocery store. Rumanos and Nazha were Badawi's two youngest siblings, Nazha being four years older than Rumanos. There was a close brother-sister relationship between the two that was rekindled and nurtured during the Mobile years and continued all their lives.[16]

Nazha and Rumanos Farchakh 1903

As the grocery store business prospered into 1904, Badawi purchased a horse and buggy. This made his peddler business much easier and more profitable than walking his routes. In addition to carrying more goods to sell and expanding his selling territory into a larger geographical area, he could deliver greater quantities of merchandise to customers in outlying areas including Baldwin County, across the Bay from Mobile proper.[17] Badawi had a wide variety of items for sale. Among his inventory was a book on comparative religion, *Rays of Light from All Lands*, which, according to the publisher's policy statement, was available only through a "duly appointed representative who has secured rights in the territory canvassed, and by paying, without deviation, the publisher's regular price of publication."[18]

By 1904 municipalities and counties across the US required peddlers to purchase licenses. Badawi bought one that year to operate in Baldwin County as "a peddler in wagon drawn by one horse or another animal."[19] The fee was $37.50, a considerable amount of money at the time especially when compared to the $25.00 cost of his horse and buggy. Fees charged for peddler licenses throughout the US were often exorbitant, in some cases running into the hundreds of dollars. Licensing ordinances were sometimes enacted by state, county and municipal governments after being lobbied by local merchants who wanted to limit, if not end, competition from itinerant peddlers. The fees charged for a peddler license in some Alabama jurisdictions were affected by at least one other factor. Under certain provisions of the Alabama constitution, revenue generated by the state from property taxes was not available to local governments. To fund education, road and bridge construction and maintenance, or other public works, local governments could generate revenue only through income taxes, bonds, or license fees. Voter reluctance to approve additional tax levies and the high interest

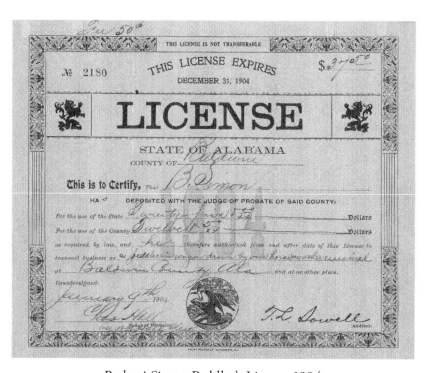

Badawi Simon Peddler's License 1904

burden of bonds led local governments to shift their revenue sources to less politically sensitive measures such as license fees.[20]

The business climate was good in Mobile, and the industrialization had brought about much construction and economic expansion. Bicycles and bowler hats were in vogue, and Mobile was current with most of the social trends of the day. However, it lacked the new and modern establishment that was breaking onto the American entertainment scene: a movie house. Seeing this as a good business opportunity, Badawi decided that Mobile was ready for one. He found a partner and an agreement was reached whereby the partner would locate and lease the facility, and Badawi would purchase the projector.[21]

At first glance, this might not appear to have been the forward thinking or innovative idea that it was. In the first years of the twentieth century, nickelodeons were springing up across the US and becoming a popular craze but there was a major limitation. Projectors of the period were the peep-hole variety that required a patron to stand close to the machine and "peep" through an opening to watch the movie. A device that enlarged images to a size that could be projected onto a screen for a large audience to see was not available in the US until 1896 when the Edison Vitascope projector was introduced. This was the machine that Badawi needed to purchase to fulfill his half of the partnership agreement and get the movie house going.

Travel arrangements were made. Badawi and Catherine left their children in the care of Rumanos and Nazha and traveled by train to Chicago. They mixed business with pleasure and spent a few days visiting local Syrian acquaintances. The Vitascope dealer instructed Badawi on the operation and maintenance of the projector, and the purchase was made. With the projector and a few spare parts plus gifts for their children the Simons returned to Mobile.[22] Here the story takes two directions. By some accounts Badawi had the first movie house in Mobile,[23] but it was unsuccessful; others maintained his partner did not or could not arrange for a facility, and the movie house never opened.[24] The consensus of those who recalled this story was that the movie house opened but was not a successful venture. After it closed down, the projector was not sold or discarded but became one of those possessions people invariably hang on to. It was seen stored in Simon homes in Mobile and later Montgomery for the next twenty years.

Badawi Simon's attempts to improve his economic status were not limited to launching a movie house. In December 1906, he acquired fifteen shares of common stock in Pacific Wireless Telegraph Company of Tacoma, Washington.[25] The term "wireless telegraph" has more than one definition, but as it applied to Pacific Wireless, it was the name given to early radio stations. At the time, the broadcast industry was barely in its early infancy. The vacuum tube, the core of radio technology until the development of the transistor in 1947, was not invented until late 1906. There were no national radio networks and no federal licensing or regulation of the nascent broadcast industry until it was placed under the jurisdiction of the Interstate Commerce Commission in 1910. As with any new scientific development, there are those who advance technology for its own sake, others who use it to build legitimate commercial enterprises, and sometimes charlatans who exploit it for illegal gain.

In May 1910, four years after Badawi's stock purchase, a plan was hatched by a holding company named Continental Wireless Telephone and Telegraph. The plan as it was explained by its officers and in its advertisements was to consolidate certain radio stations across the US and inaugurate a transcontinental commercial radio network. It was

Pacific Wireless Stock Certificate 1906

a heady project for its day. Among the several companies Continental acquired was Pacific Wireless. Meanwhile, in Washington, D.C., the Post Office Department launched a campaign to crack down on the sale of unlisted stocks. In the process, investigations headed by the Postmaster General targeted firms using the US mails for fraudulent commerce, and Continental's professed ambitions were exposed as a scam. When all was said and done, the new holding company came crashing down and Pacific Wireless with it.[26] Whether Badawi ever received a dividend check from Pacific Wireless before its entanglement with Continental is not known and perhaps it might have been a good investment if the station had remained independent of Continental Wireless. In the end, he lost the value of his investment but that was the extent of his financial liability.

Even when he was chasing other business opportunities, Badawi was careful to nurture his peddling business. But it had its limitations. Beginning in the period around 1905-1910, the peddler business had reached its zenith.[27] It was still a profitable vocation, but times were changing. Local stores began to expand their inventories due to improved means of transportation, especially rail, and mail-order catalog companies advertised a broader selection of merchandise than what peddlers could offer. Badawi might have realized that times were changing and he needed to change the way he operated his business or even seek another means of livelihood. Whatever he decided to do, he could count on Catherine's support and abilities. She had demonstrated that she was fully capable of operating a grocery store, but the income was not sufficient to meet all the needs of a growing family. The condition of the national economy did not help as prices increased fifty percent faster than wages between 1897 and 1909, a condition that directly affected the peddler business. In an effort to remedy his economic problems,

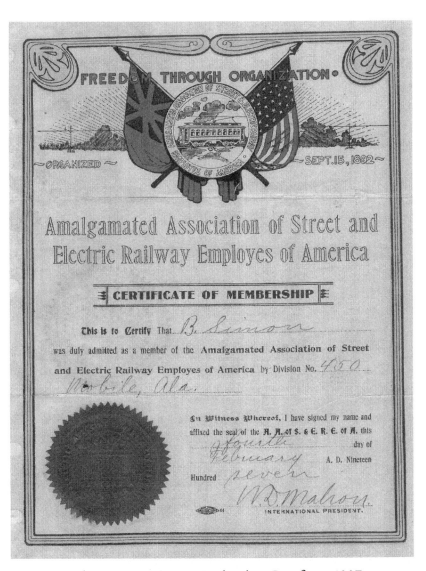

Badawi Simon Union Membership Certificate 1907

Badawi veered from his peddler trade and, in February 1907, became a member of the Amalgamated Association of Street and Electric Railway Employees of America, also known as the Carmen's Union.[28]

In 1893 electric trolleys began operation in Mobile. At the time, the transit system included the new cars plus existing mule-drawn trolleys that remained in service until the last one was retired in 1902. The trolley routes served the areas in and around Government, Conti, and Dauphine Streets. As a member of the Carmen's Union, Badawi went to work as a motorman for the system's franchise holder, Mobile Light & Railroad Company. For about a year, he worked ten-hour shifts at a wage of twenty-five cents an hour. The streetcar job was unique to Syrians in general and Badawi Simon in particular. It was unusual for a Syrian to be a union member in the South as well as to be working for hourly wages. The time Badawi spent with the Mobile transit system was the only time he worked as an employee for hourly wages.

Toward the end of 1908, the Simons came to the conclusion that to prosper economically they needed to relocate away from Mobile.[29] In the nine years they had been there, more and more Syrians and members of other ethnic groups had migrated to South Alabama and the Gulf Coast. Many had entered the peddler trade. Each new immigrant was eager to acquire some of the riches they had heard about from peddler success stories reaching the old country. As Mobile continued to grow, competition increased and the Simons' "mom and pop" grocery store became stagnant. In December, they sold the lease on the store, and the family, including Rumanos, moved to Birmingham.[30]

Although Mobile was behind Badawi Simon, an incident occurred there that followed him for the rest of his life. It concerned his sister Nazha and her husband Mansour Leon.

Nazha and Mansour were married in 1898 during the time the Simons were in Mount Lebanon. A few months later, the newlyweds immigrated to the US with Mobile as their destination. Once in Mobile one of the first Syrians they looked up was Faris Hawie. The young couple planned to establish themselves by working as route peddlers, and they needed the help and support services of a peddler outfitter. At the time, Faris and Mansour were both eighteen years old. Nazha was seventeen. Faris provided the couple with living quarters and helped them improve their spoken English. Soon Mansour, sometimes with Nazha at his side, was peddling merchandise supplied by Faris from his dry goods store but within a few months it became necessary for her to end her traveling with Mansour. She was pregnant, and, after the birth of her first son Wadih in 1899, she needed to be at home.[31]

Within a few years, something went wrong in their marriage. There were no glaring signs that anything was awry, or, at least if there was, nothing was openly discussed. Whatever the problems might have been, it is likely that their genesis was partially linked to the fact that they were not living in Mount Lebanon. Had they remained there the marriage would have survived perhaps unhappily but persevered nonetheless. There were several reasons for this.

Families in the old country lived within close proximity to each other both physically and metaphorically. There were few if any secrets among kin, and a series of checks and balances operated as a corrective mechanism to resolve disputes including marital spats. In the end, the patriarchal father would intervene and his word was final. Marriage in Lebanon is strictly a religious matter and standing behind a Maronite father's moral authority was the ever-present power of the Church. Its traditions and marriage laws made it virtually impossible to dissolve the sacrament of matrimony through divorce.

In the US, none of the old country corrective mechanisms or coercive institutions existed. Mansour and Nazha had a problem, and she evidently came to the conclusion that she would take matters in hand and solve it in her own way. Whatever actions, if any, Mansour might have been planning or taking are not known. The occasion to tell her brother what she was about to do occurred one evening in early 1906. The Leons and Simons lived within walking distance of each other, and, on this particular evening, Nazha was in the Simon home where she had brought her son Wadih to give him and the Simon's younger children their evening baths.[32] When the chore was finished, the children were dressed for bed. Badawi was at home having returned that afternoon from Baldwin County. He was sitting at the kitchen table going over paper work pertaining to his business activities paying little attention to the goings on around him. Nazha walked up to the table and said she needed to talk with him. When he looked up, she faced him squarely and announced she was going to divorce Mansour Leon and marry Faris Hawie.[33]

Divorce was not unheard of in 1906, and divorce rates had been gradually increasing since about 1895 due to several factors including industrialization and the gradual liberalization of social attitudes. By 1906 the national divorce rate stood at about eight percent, a comparatively low number when contrasted with the contemporary rate that hovers around fifty percent. Nonetheless, alongside the statistics of divorce, there was the social aspect. In 1906 it carried a stigma often associated rightly or wrongly with adultery.

Badawi was a conservative man in manner and attitude. His only known vice was smoking cigarettes which he rolled himself with his favorite tobacco, King Bee. He did not drink alcoholic beverages, and, on those rare occasions when he appeared to do so, he only touched the glass to his lips to be sociable. When asked why he did not drink, he would state simply that he "didn't like the stuff."[34] He tolerated the idiosyncrasies of the people he dealt with in business which he had to do in his line of work, but there were limits to his indulgence when it came to family matters.

Nazha was twenty-five years old, Badawi eight years older. Brother and sister had been raised in the same home in the same traditional society, and both understood the rules of personal conduct taught by family and church. In a way, Badawi was a sort of family semi-patriarch, if that concept can be applied to an extended Syrian family living in the US. Nazha was well aware of his strong religious convictions, and, until that eventful day in 1906, she had not collided with his sensitivities. She no doubt anticipated a negative response from him but even with an understanding of her brother's traditional values, morality, and religious beliefs, she might not have been sufficiently prepared for what actually occurred. As a young child, Sy Forshee witnessed the scene and years later said that when Nazha told Badawi she planned to divorce Mansour and marry Faris "all hell broke loose." Badawi's face turned red, and he lost his temper, flying into a rage the likes of which Sy said he never saw or heard of before or since.[35]

Catherine was sitting in a nearby chair sewing and looked up when Badawi sprang from his chair. She watched and said nothing possibly because she was seeing a side of her husband she did not know existed. After all, this was the same man she had laughingly said would rather jump in the lake than get into an argument. But Nazha's disclosure trampled on too many immutable personal and religious beliefs and old country traditions. Her intention to divorce her husband was bad enough, but to turn around and marry another man implied more than Badawi could bear. Whatever explanation she might have wanted to offer was of no interest to him, and the details of her problem made no difference.[36] He could not and would not condone nor tolerate what he deemed scandalous conduct by any family member and certainly not from his sister. In the midst of his rage, Badawi pointed toward the door and shouted "get out and go live with Hawie."[37] She hesitated for a brief moment and then silently turned away from her brother, picked up her son, and walked out. The scene was all over in less than a minute. But the emotional havoc unleashed during those few moments carried far-reaching consequences. An irreparable estrangement ripped Badawi and Nazha apart. It was never fully mended.

Whatever Badawi might have done to intervene in the affair is not known, but, as it turned out, Nazha did not divorce Mansour; Mansour divorced her, and, in the process, she gained custody of seven-year-old Wadih. Once the legal proceedings were concluded and the divorce granted, Nazha married Faris Hawie who legally adopted Wadih.[38] The young boy's surname was changed from Leon to Hawie and he remained Wadih Faris Hawie the rest of his life. The marriage of Nazha and Faris lasted until Faris's death in 1932. Mansour continued to operate his grocery store. After the Simons moved to Montgomery, Badawi would lodge with Mansour when he traveled to Mobile on business. They remained very close friends. Catherine sometimes traveled with Badawi to Mobile and visited her many friends who lived there. In 1910, Mansour's life changed again.

The previous year an immigrant from Ehden named Salima Soutou came to Mobile. Known as Selma Soto in the US, her mother was one of Badawi's aunts. After a relatively short courtship, she and Mansour were married on September 23, 1910. According to an account told years later by her daughter Annie, Selma did not know Mansour was a divorced man. For their marriage ceremony, they went to Saint John's

Episcopal Church in Mobile. Because the name Saint John was part of the church name, Selma later said she thought it was a Catholic Church.[39] Mansour was legally divorced in the eyes of the state but was not permitted to remarry in the Catholic Church or Maronite Rite. Selma did not know she was entering into an ecclesiastically problematic marriage. The idea that anything was irregular in Mansour's standing with the church is said to have never crossed her mind. Sometime later when she discovered that Mansour was a divorced man, she was quite upset.[40] But the marriage endured. Over a period of fourteen years, she and Mansour became parents to six children: Marie, Annie, George, Michael, William, and John.

With the exception of his early years as a route peddler and his work as a carpenter with Louisville & Nashville Railroad during the Great War, Mansour made his living as a grocery store owner.[41] He was not known to have been in bad health, but in 1924 he continued to suffer from reoccurring symptoms of malaria. Where or when he contracted the illness is not known. According to an account given by his daughter Annie Leon Stauter, he was working in his store on August 25, 1924. Things were proceeding in a routine manner when he was visited in the late afternoon by an acquaintance who owed him money. The visitor had stopped by to tell Mansour that he was unable to repay the money on the date previously agreed upon and asked for additional time. In the course of the conversation, the visitor asked Mansour if his malaria was still a problem. When Mansour said it was, the visitor offered him a small matchbox. In it was a single pill. The visitor told Mansour it would be beneficial. Without a great deal of questioning on his part Mansour tool the pill and swallowed it. Soon after, his visitor departed.[42]

A short time later, Mansour began to walk erratically as if in search of something. Suddenly he was seized with involuntary muscular convulsions. He fell to the floor in what appeared to be an epileptic fit. His speech became incoherent. Selma called for an ambulance and Mansour was taken to the hospital. The doctors were evidently unable to diagnose or treat his convulsions which continued throughout the night until 3:30 a.m., when he died.[43] He was forty-four years old. No autopsy was performed, and, if there was any suspicion of foul play, no investigation was made.[44] On August 28, services were held at the Cathedral of the Immaculate Conception. Badawi and Catherine who were living in Montgomery by this time drove down for the services and stayed in Mobile for a few days. Mansour was Badawi's first cousin, their mothers were sisters, and Selma's mother was Warda Mkhayel Farchakh, Badawi's aunt. Whether the debtor who gave Mansour the would-be curative pill eventually paid Selma the money he owed Mansour is not known.[45]

Selma was forty-one years old when Mansour died and was fully capable of operating the grocery store. But there were limitations to what she could do alone. This was especially true when it came to operating a business that provided her family's livelihood and at the same time taking care of six young children. Her oldest child, Marie, was thirteen but the other five children were twelve or younger. She took the course she thought best and sent the four boys, George ten, Michael eight, William six and John, still a toddler, to live at the Brothers of the Sacred Heart Boys Orphanage in Mobile. Marie and her twelve-year-old sister, Annie, remained at home. After a short time at the orphanage, John, not quite two years old and unhappy being away from home was brought back to live with his mother and sisters.[46]

The orphanage or asylum as it was also termed when the Leon boys were enrolled was known as the Boy's Industrial School. It was a Catholic institution operated by the Brothers of the Sacred Heart, a religious order founded in France in 1821 by Father Andre Coindre. The order's charter was to provide a practical and spiritual education to children throughout the world. In 1846, Bishop Michael Portier, himself French by birth and the organizer of the Catholic Diocese of Mobile, asked Brother Polycarp, Superior General of the Order, to establish a boy's orphanage in Mobile. In January 1847, Brother Polycarp answered Bishop Portier's request by sending from France to Mobile five missionary brothers who established the first Brothers of the Sacred Heart orphanage outside France. By the 1920s, when Mansour Leon's sons were enrolled there, it was a thriving and progressive orphanage and school for boys.[47]

Birmingham and Katherine Shakra

The Simons' move to Birmingham and the labor shortage in the railroad industry proved to be a significant turning point in Rumanos Simon's life. He revised the spelling of his last name, sometimes using Simhan which is pronounced similar to the Arabic pronunciation of Semaan. In early 1909, at age twenty-four, he married Susan Boulos el Gerr el Douaihy, a young Syrian-American woman from the Douaihy family of Mount Lebanon. Their first child, Farid, was born within a year.[1] There was no Maronite Church in Birmingham at the time of Rumanos and Susan's wedding or when Farid was born. But, in 1910 this ended with the founding of Saint Elias parish, the first Maronite Church in the south. All the Simhan children born in the US after Farid were baptized there.[2]

In the local job market, one of the firms that looked to immigrants as a solution to their labor shortage problem was the Louisville & Nashville Railroad. Rumanos learned of an opening and applied for the job. He was hired and eventually became a machinist in the railroad's car repair shop where he worked with another Syrian immigrant and friend Albert George who came to the US from Lebanon in 1905.[3]

While on the job, Rumanos was involved in a near-fatal accident that occurred while he was standing between two stationary rail cars working on a coupler mechanism. Unexpectedly, one car rolled toward the other trapping him and partially crushing his lower abdomen. The result was a severely damaged kidney. He was rushed to a hospital where an examination revealed the injury was life threatening. Apparently, the doctors were convinced Rumanos had nothing to lose if they operated which they proceeded to do. In a delicate surgical procedure, the damaged kidney was removed, reportedly among the first if not *the* first successful nephrectomy performed in Alabama.[4] In today's world of advanced surgery and transplants, an operation of this sort might be viewed as a somewhat routine procedure, but, in the early 1900s, there was no modern anesthesia, pain medication, or vascular clamps. Also absent were sulfa drugs to counter infection, blood transfusions, intravenous techniques, and stringent sterilization methods. The fact that the operation was successful and Rumanos did not die from infection or loss of blood was no doubt due to the combination of medical skill by a long-forgotten surgical team and Rumanos' inordinate personal strength.[5]

Sometime after recovering from his accident, Rumanos went into business and opened a restaurant in downtown Birmingham. He operated it through 1916. By the time the US declared war on Germany in April 1917, he and his family had moved from Birmingham to Detroit, Michigan. Several members of his wife's family already lived there, and some of them worked in factories producing war materiel. In compliance with the newly enacted Selective Service legislation, Rumanos registered with the Detroit draft board on June 5, 1917 using the name Roman Simon. He listed his job as a machinist at Dodge

Brothers, which was under government contract to manufacture vehicles for the army.[6]

During the time the Simons lived in Birmingham, Badawi tried his hand at wholesale merchandising and at the same time acquired a financial interest in a neighborhood restaurant. Neither venture met his expectations, so he and his family stayed in Birmingham less than a year.[7] During the time they were there, they had the opportunity to renew their acquaintance with one of Badawi's cousins whom he had not seen since before his and Catherine's first emigration two decades earlier.

Katherine Numnum Zataney had a history with the Farchakh family in Mount Lebanon and the Simon family in the US that spanned a period of almost seventy years. Her kinship to Badawi Simon was through her mother who was a Farchakh. Katherine was an imposing figure to see or meet, not fat but rather a big woman close to six feet tall. Among her personal characteristics were independence, assertiveness, a quick sense of humor, and good business judgment which she had used to considerable success in the US. In leisure moments she often smoked a *narghili*, the Turkish water pipe.

While in her teens, Katherine married a cousin named Assad Zataney whose mother, like Katherine's, was a Farchakh.[8] From this marriage came two sons, Salim (b.1889) and Mehsen (b.1892). Sometime around the time of Mehsen's birth, Assad died. Finding herself widowed with two young children, Katherine decided to go ahead with the emigration she and Assad had planned. Because of the uncertainties she might encounter, she decided to temporarily leave her two sons in Lebanon in the care of Semaan Mkhayel and Warda Farchakh.[9]

In 1895, she arrived in the US and initially settled in Waterbury, Connecticut where members of the Numnum family and a growing community of Lebanese immigrants lived. Within a year, she married a peddler and part-time carpenter named Kahlil Shakra who had immigrated from Zgharta in 1892. In 1896, her oldest son, Salim, joined her and her new husband.[10] While is secondary school Salim became an accomplished athlete and won several awards in boxing and wrestling. Mehsen, the youngest son, elected to remain in Lebanon with Semaan Mkhayel and Warda until sometime after 1910.[11]

Katherine gave birth to her third child and only daughter in 1897. The baby girl was given the traditional name Salimi but was known as Sara. To the Simon family and their descendants she was "Cousin Sara," one of the most delightful people around, intelligent, conversant, and very pleasant.

Shortly after the turn of the century, the Shakras moved to Birmingham. Katherine continued to work as a peddler. But she had a better future in mind for her son, Salim. Peddling was an honorable trade, but it had its limitations. Some Syrians peddled all their working lives and made a good living. For others it served as a means of upward economic mobility. Katherine used her resources to help her son advance to a professional career by arranging for him to be apprenticed by an itinerant optician named Doctor Henry Barson.[12] Local medical schools later established across the US were not readily available for institutional training and learning trades and professions was oftentimes gained through apprenticeship.

Working under the tutelage of Henry Barson, Salim, which translates as Samuel, changed his given name to Sam and dropped Zataney as his surname. In its place, he adopted Henry Barson's surname and became known as Sam A. Barson. Adopting his mentor's surname made Sam's name sound less foreign and more "American," a goal sought by many Syrians. Sam maintained the middle initial "A" which stood for his father's name, Assad. After completing his apprenticeship, he relocated to Montgomery. In 1909, he married Monzora Moses, the oldest daughter of Mike and Rose Moses and, within a year, was working fulltime as an optometrist. The couple lived with her parents on Julian Street in Montgomery.[13] After Sam's brother Mehsen immigrated to the US and changed his given name to Michael, he too was apprenticed as an optometrist by Sam. To avoid direct competition with each other, the brothers divided Alabama into two territories. Sam worked in Montgomery and the surrounding counties while Michael worked in Birmingham and areas to the west and north.

Montgomery

During the years before the construction of a bypass and the commercial migration from downtown, much of the business activity in and around Montgomery centered on Court Square and its adjacent streets. Those that converged at the Court Square fountain came in at oblique angles but most of the others were at right angles to each other. The main street, Dexter Avenue, extended from the fountain to the east a dozen blocks or so to Bainbridge Street. Had it continued a few more feet, it would have collided with the steps of the Alabama State Capitol building.

Along this thoroughfare that was originally cobble stoned before being paved over with asphalt were all kinds of establishments: shops, churches, professional offices, snack bars, restaurants, and the YMCA. There were also department stores, the most well known being the Montgomery Fair. Whatever a consumer might want was usually available at one or more of the Dexter Avenue stores. Some of the businesses were owned by immigrants with non-English, Irish, Welsh, or Scottish names who gradually emerged as a dynamic force in Montgomery's business and cultural life.

According to Montgomery historian Mary Ann Neeley, there is no record of exactly when the first 19th century immigrants arrived in Montgomery. It is known that in the 1840s, several French and Italian-speaking families arrived from Corsica, the island birthplace of Napoleon Bonaparte. The same decade saw the arrival of German Jews. Later, Alsatian Jews came in the aftermath of the 1870-71 Franco-Prussian War. But not all immigrants coming to Montgomery were from Western Europe. Neeley identified a man named Speridon Cassimus as Montgomery's first Greek immigrant. He arrived in the late 1880s and was followed by a number of other Greek families.[1] According to individual arrival dates recorded in US Census reports, Syrians and other emigrants from Ottoman ruled lands began to settle in Montgomery in the early 1890s.

The Simons arrived in Montgomery in late 1908. Birmingham had not been to Badawi's liking after ventures in a wholesale dry goods business and later a small restaurant. Their first home in Montgomery was at 10 King Street. They had been there for only a few weeks when, on Ash Wednesday, February 24, 1909, Frances was born. Forty days later on Easter Sunday when she was baptized, her godparents were Assad Barad and the wife of Hanna Boulos el Gerr el Doueihy known better as Hanna Gerr.[2] Frances was the fourth Simon daughter (two older sisters, Jamileh and Saidi, had died young) and the second daughter named Jamileh after one of her deceased sisters. Naming a new born child after a deceased sibling or departed relative is traditional in the Middle East dating from antiquity. Jamileh's baptismal name was Frances and, until her marriage in 1929, she was known as Frances B. Simon.[3]

Sometime in 1911 the Simons moved from King Street to a larger home at 207 South Bainbridge. Here, their last child George was born August 31, 1912. His traditional name was Badih, "pretty baby," but he was known mostly by his baptismal name, George, or to family members and friends as Buster, a nickname dating from childhood. Prior to George's baptism, all the US-born Simon children received the sacrament in church ceremonies in the Latin Rite. There were no Maronite Churches in New Orleans, Jacksonville, Mobile, or Montgomery where the children were born. Johnny was the exception having been was born in Ehden and baptized into the Maronite Rite in Zgharta. In recording his son George's birth and baptism, Badawi Simon wrote in his Bible, "He [George] was baptized in ninety minutes."[4] In later years, this led to speculation that there might have been some concern about the new-born boy's survival in the first minutes of his life. Possibly fearing that the child might die without being baptized, Badawi telephoned for a priest to come immediately and administer the sacrament. No other explanation has emerged to explain why George alone among his siblings was baptized at home immediately after his birth and not baptized later in a more formal church ceremony.

Assad Barad, Badawi Simon's long-time friend, was George's godfather. His godmother was recorded as "Regina, wife of Faris Dagher el Ghabala" from Kesseroun, an administrative district in Lebanon north of Beirut.[5] Until at least 1930, this last child of Badawi and Catherine was known as George Simon. Sometime around 1930, he replaced the Simon surname with Farshee but continued using the middle initial "B." Like some of his siblings, he maintained that it stood for Bernard which was said to be a translation of Badawi. However, the etymologies of these two names do not support the claim that one is a translation of the other but adopted names among Syrian immigrants were more the rule than the exception.[6]

Mary Simon holding George with Frances and Sy 1913

Zaki Azar and The American Hat Company

The influx of immigrants to the US and Montgomery continued during the first decades of the twentieth century until legal barriers erected by Congressional legislation during the 1920s brought it to an end. But in the years before the Great War, among the new arrivals to Montgomery was a young man who was to have a profound affect on the Simon family. His name was Zaki Azar.

Zaki Naoum Azar was born in Antioch, Syria on June 25, 1890.[1] His father, Naoum Azar and mother, Catherine Elian, were parents to eight children; daughters, Miryana, Zakia, Jamileh, Emily and Badiya and sons George, Zaki and Gabriel. By most accounts Zaki and Gabriel were educated in Constantinople[2] but one story suggests that the two boys were schooled in Greece because the Ottoman regime prohibited Christian schools in Constantinople.[3]

George, the oldest of the Azar brothers and Zaki immigrated to the US in1904. Immigration authorities at Ellis Island listed Zaki's profession as "smith" possibly used at the time as a catch-all term for a non-specialized worker. He had in his pockets a total of eight dollars. The immigrant registry acknowledged that the fourteen year old could read and write English but did not mention his penchant for languages.[4] He was conversant in four others beside English.

Once in the US the Azar brothers lived and worked for a time in New York. By 1912, Zack, as he was also known, had relocated to Montgomery where he was employed as a tailor at W.C. Stuckey.[5] At the time he was living in a rented room on North Perry. The following year he changed jobs and went with Alex Rice's store on North Court. Another change occurred when he began renting a room in the home of Badawi Simon and his family at 207 South Bainbridge. This was the beginning of his relationship with the Simon family that continued for the rest of his life. While living in the Simon home he fell in love with their oldest daughter, Mary. The attraction was mutual and in September 1914 they were married; he was twenty-four, she was twenty. Consistent with old country tradition and probably for practical economic purposes as well, furniture and clothes were rearranged in the Simon home and the Azar newlyweds set up their own apartment.

At the time Zaki was working as a tailor at W. C. Stuckey in 1912, two enterprising merchants, Raphael Cohen and Isaac Hasson, opened a men's hat and clothing store at 32-1/2 Commerce. Operating under the company name of Cohen and Hasson, the business prospered. Two years later, Hasson ended his partnership with Cohen and established himself as Isaac Hasson, the Hatter at 211-1/2 Dexter Avenue, about a block from where Zaki worked. When Hasson left the company he and Cohen had founded, Cohen renamed it the German Hat Company. In 1916 Raphael Cohen took on a new partner named Joe Toronto. The two partners expanded their business by opening a second store at 26 North Court next to one of the entrances to the Montgomery Fair. The original location on Commerce remained for another year.[6]

Zaki Azar and Mary Simon Marriage Photograph 1914

As the German Hat Company was making its place in the local market in 1913, Zaki Azar left W.C. Stuckey and went to work at Alex Rice's store where he remained until September 1914 when he again changed jobs and went with Hurley Brothers. Zaki's brother George joined him in 1915. The following year, Zaki entered into partnership with Isaac Hasson. The name of the business was changed to Hasson & Azar and moved to 121 Dexter. Zaki's association with Isaac Hasson turned out to be one of those career-enhancing events that broadened his business experience and knowledge. Until that time, Zaki had worked as a tailor but at Hasson and Azar he learned the hat business from manufacturing to cleaning.[7]

The year the US entered the Great War, 1917, Hasson and Azar expanded into the space over their shop and next door into 119-1/2 Dexter Avenue. Part of the expansion led to the opening of a separate venture, the Post Office Lunch restaurant adjacent to the hat shop. Its day-to-day operation was managed by a man named J.B. Whiting, but records of the time listed Zaki Azar as the owner.[8]

Back over on North Court, Joe Toronto bought out Raphael Cohen's interest in the German Hat Company and became its sole owner. The influx of personnel for training at nearby military facilities provided a stimulus for the economy of Montgomery and career adjustments were occurring all over the place. George Azar left his job at Hurley Brothers and joined Hasson and Azar.[9] Then, shortly after the 1918 armistice was signed ending the Great War, Zaki put into motion one of the most important business decisions of his life. He planned to sell his interest in Hasson and Azar and have his own store. Negotiations were concluded in early February 1919 when Joe Toronto and Zaki came to terms for the sale of what had been named the German Hat Company.[10] As the war in Europe intensified and US ships increasingly became targets for submarines, anti-German sentiment and patriotic zeal turned violent. After the US declaration of war there were incidents of German-American businesses being attacked and in some cases destroyed. As anti-German fervor intensified books written in German were burned and the musical works of Bach and Wagner no longer performed. German shepherds became "police dogs," German measles became "liberty measles" and the town of Berlin, Maryland was renamed Brunswick. The fallout from these events led some families with German surnames to change them to more English-sounding ones. Even the names of certain foods were changed; sauerkraut became "liberty cabbage" and hamburger was renamed "Salisbury steak."[11] In the frenzied political climate of 1917, Joe Toronto apparently determined it was in his best interest to rename the German Hat Company. It became the American Hat Company.[12]

Under the terms of sale, Zaki paid Toronto a total of $4,000.00, the equivalent of $51,600.00 in 2008 dollars. After a cash down payment of $1,500.00, the balance was carried by Toronto to be paid off with ten promissory notes of $250.00 each that fell due on the first of the month beginning in April 1919. The purchase included "all store fixtures, showcases, mirrors, tables and chairs ... one iron safe ... and all tools and merchandise." Attached to the sale document were six sheets listing the inventory Zaki had purchased. The lease on the building was transferred as well as some adjacent space that was sub-let.[13] On February 6, 1919, the day after the sale was formalized, Zaki Azar went to work in his own business. He was twenty-nine years old and had been in the US for fifteen years.

Rheumatism, a Restaurant and a New Career

About the time Zaki Azar was becoming a member of the Simon household, the first recorded instance of a health related issue pertaining to Badawi Simon surfaced. Prior to 1913, there are no known records or comments one way or the other about his personal health. But he apparently had at least one known physical malady. On May 27 of that year, Doctor M.L. Wood, chairman of the Montgomery County Board of Health, wrote a letter certifying that

> *Mr. B. Simon suffers with rheumatism (chronic) and is physically unable to do manual labor and I would recommend that he be granted license to peddle.*

In addition to Doctor Wood, the letter was signed by six members of the Board of Health.[1] The next day Probate Judge J.B. Gaston, acting on the Health Board's recommendation, ruled that "B. Simon is authorized to peddle in any county in this state without a license."[2] Decades later, when interviewed for this story, no one could offer any details about the extent or severity of Badawi's chronic rheumatism. However, there was a definite economic benefit to Judge Gaston's ruling. Authorization to peddle statewide without a license for each county substantially reduced the cost of doing business. It had the effect of transforming the entire state of Alabama into Badawi Simon's market place

Within a year, Badawi's economic situation improved to the extent that he purchased a Model T Ford.[3] This provided more mobility, and his travel throughout the state became more extensive. In the conduct of his business activities, he seemed to be on a constant lookout for new opportunities. Two of his friends, Mike Moses, the father-in-law of Sam Barson and Badawi's friend Assad Barad, both operated restaurants.[4] As his peddling business became more profitable, he once again accumulated sufficient surplus capital for another venture. He decided to try his hand as a restaurateur. With fellow Syrian immigrant Hanna Jurr (Hanna el Jurr el Doueihy), they opened a restaurant in the Bogue Homa district. Hanna operated the business with Badawi as the silent partner.[5]

Bogue Homa, named for the red water flowing from what is now Genetta Creek, had become home to thousands of African-Americans in the late 19th century and was a town unto its own. Located on South Decatur outside the city limits, commercial establishments sprang up to serve the customers of Baggett's Blacksmith Shop. Farmers and farm hands from all around Montgomery County came to Baggett's to get their horses and mules shod and often stayed overnight in nearby hotels. There were no fixed hours for some businesses, and at least one grocery store stayed open all night. A farmer's trip to Bogue Homa was also an opportunity to shop in Montgomery's stores.[6]

In 1915, it was at its peak of fame and seemed like a good place to open a restaurant. The dynamic little area attracted a great number of visitors all of them potential café customers. Badawi and Hanna's café operated from 6:00 a.m. to 8:00 p.m. It was not an elaborate or glamorous art deco style diner, but rather a simple room with bare wooden floors with a combination of a half dozen counter stools and a few tables and chairs. During its busy hours, it could accommodate a total of about twenty patrons who were served traditional southern meals. There was talk of longer opening hours, but that never happened. A fourteen hour day was too long as it was. With a continuous flow of customers, the venture was lively and financially successful. The two partners operated the restaurant for about two years, after which time they sold it and divided the profits. It was said that the sale of the venture gave each partner a reasonable return on their respective investment.[7]

During the years of the Great War, Badawi Simon's business activities were advancing in a reasonably profitable manner but he began to be interested in establishing himself in a more professional vocation. In 1915, at age 42, he became a naturalized US citizen and decided to transition from peddling to optometry.[8] He had followed Sam Barson's promising career as an optometrist, and he found it appealing. Many aspects of Sam's work complemented Badawi's sales experience, such as traveling and effective customer contact. He and Sam spent considerable time discussing its benefits. Once Badawi reconciled himself to a career change, Sam agreed to apprentice him. After several months of training, Badawi too began practicing optometry. Starting in 1916, Sam and Badawi operated independently of each other and agreed on the establishment of separate territories: Sam worked north of Montgomery and Badawi went south as far as Geneva, Alabama on the Florida State line and Mobile.[9]

There was no licensing or regulation of optometrists in Alabama until legislation was passed in 1919. Those practicing that year and beyond were registered by "limited certificates." Sam Barson was issued License number L-1, Badawi Simon License number 121.[10] Because there was no state examination board or other qualification requirements, an optometrist's proficiency was established through testimonial letters written by satisfied patients. Badawi had at least one such letter dated June 20, 1916. Addressed *To Whom It May Concern* it read:

> *This is to certify that Dr. B. Simon fitted glasses for me several months ago and they are entirely satisfactory. I have tried several opticians in Mobile and elsewhere and can conscientiously recommend this man to my friends as a thoroughly competent optician.*

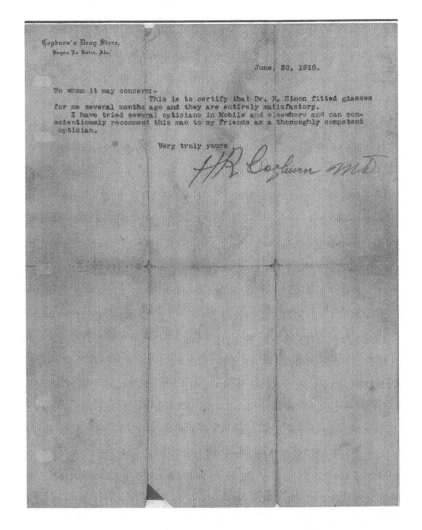

The letter, written on stationery of Cogburn's Drug Store in Bayou La Batre, Alabama, was signed H.R. Cogburn, M.D.[11] Badawi carried the neatly folded letter with him and based upon an examination of the original document, one might conclude that it was folded and unfolded many times.

There is no record of the processes Badawi Simon utilized to transform himself from peddler to optometrist, nor is there any indication that he walked away from his peddler business one day and suddenly appeared the next as an optometrist. His first concern was providing for his family. He had done this as a peddler for most of his time in the US. By 1916, when he received Doctor Cogburn's endorsement letter, he was forty-three years old and had developed customers and commercial contacts throughout central and south Alabama. To suggest that he suddenly turned away from what had been a sustaining livelihood to a new-found endeavor is not realistic nor would it have been a responsible decision on his part to have done so. It is more than likely he worked his optometry practice into his peddler business and for a while did both.[12] Once his practice was in full swing, Badawi moved to a higher economic tier, although he followed the same path of upward mobility adhered to by most Syrian immigrants. Many of them began as route peddlers and, with accumulated funds, subsequently opened stores, usually selling dry goods, notions, or groceries. Badawi followed this progression but advanced to optometry rather than the retailing or wholesaling of merchandise.

Part of the training he had acquired from Sam Barson included techniques of eyeglass construction. In the first phase of his practice, Sam provided Badawi with eyeglass components. Once he was established on his own and the need for Sam's supervision lessened, Badawi opened an account with American Optical Company in Montgomery where he purchased his supply of lenses, frames, and other related items. Among the items he traveled with were "factory made" glasses and, if he had the correct lens and frame combination for a patient, he would fill the need on the spot. Sometimes he fabricated custom glasses at home, and on some evenings he could be seen working at the kitchen table gluing a half-moon shaped magnifying glass to a lens to make bifocals.[13] Charges for his services were paid in cash or barter, and it was not unusual for him to come home with chickens, eggs, various fruits and vegetables, and, on at least one occasion, a goat.[14] Badawi continued to travel extensively as he had in his peddler days. He knew a lot of people to call on but his efforts were focused, better defined and more financially rewarding than route peddling.

The financial rewards and personal satisfaction of practicing optometry enjoyed by Sam Barson and his brother Michael Zataney coupled with his own enthusiasm for his new profession led Badawi Simon to encourage Aziz to join him in his business.[15] One of the medical schools that taught optometry at the time was Jenner Medical College in Chicago. Aziz agreed to his father's proposal, and in 1916 Badawi funded Aziz's enrollment at Jenner for the 1916-1917 school term.[16] On one of the enrollment forms, Aziz's name appears as Sim B. Faarshee (*sic*), the first known time a version of the Farshee surname was used.[17] The text books Aziz bought for his course work included the *Pocket Ophthalmic Dictionary and Encyclopedia* and *The Practical Phrenologist: A Compendium of Phreno-Organic Science*.[18]

The Great War

When the Great War erupted in August 1914, many in Europe imagined it would be over in a matter of months. The weeks leading up to this cataclysmic event saw crowds of people gather in the streets of Berlin and Paris clamoring *for* war. Young men in Great Britain and Germany delayed their fall school enrollments preferring to join the army in anticipation of a quick, glorious victory. They imagined returning home after a few weeks of war and adventure as heroes in time to register for the spring term. Each side was blinded by the illusion that the other would be quickly defeated.[1] In the four years of conflict that followed, millions of people would be affected including the Syrians of Mount Lebanon and Alabama.

The belligerents were organized into two opposing camps, the Entente Powers or Allies: Great Britain, France and Russia versus the Central Powers led by Germany and Austria-Hungary. Most of Europe was almost immediately drawn into the fray, but the Ottoman Empire appeared to sit on the sidelines, declaring a policy of armed neutrality. In early November, the charade ended, and the fully mobilized Turks entered the war casting their lot with the Central Powers. Unbeknown to the Allies, Germany and Turkey had signed a secret alliance on August 2, 1914, two days before the first guns of August were fired.[2]

On the Western Front, the best laid military plans for a decisive victory proved to be wanting, and the conflict was quickly transformed into a monstrous war of unprecedented butchery and horror. As the New Year of 1915 dawned, the optimism for a short and relatively painless conflict had vanished. The Western Front was anything but all quiet. According to journalist and historian Walter Millis, British and French soldiers were being killed at the rate of 5,000 a day. War maps reflected less and less movement of armies as the war shifted from broad battlefield maneuvers to the stalemate of trench warfare. The Allies began to get desperate for a breakthrough. Too many men coming out of their trenches and going "over the top" were being killed, and British and French generals and politicians could point to little if anything to justify the cost in lives, pounds sterling, and francs. In an attempt to deflect the deadly efficient German war machine and draw enemy men and materiel away from the Western Front, Great Britain's War Cabinet devised a plan to attack Turkey on the Gallipoli Peninsula, the presumed soft underbelly of the Ottoman State. Once it was secured, according to the plan, the Royal Navy would breach the Dardanelles Strait and steam unencumbered into the Sea of Marmara to bombard and capture Constantinople. The Ottoman Empire would be forced to capitulate and sign an armistice.[3]

While the world's attention was focused on the Western Front and Gallipoli, another man-made tragedy was unfolding in the Eastern Mediterranean. When Turkey entered the war, Great Britain and France imposed a naval blockade of all Ottoman ports including those on the Syrian coast. Mount Lebanon and Syria were not technically at war with the Allies, but they were Ottoman provinces and, as such, were considered belligerent territories. The purpose of the blockade was to sever all maritime trade between Greater Syria and Ottoman allies and cut off goods of any kind from neutral countries. Nothing was permitted through the blockade including mail, the life-line for remittances from abroad to relatives and friends in Mount Lebanon and Syria. Everything destined for Syria including food was declared contraband. The Allies hoped to starve the Ottomans into submission, but the blockade's effect went far beyond harming the Turks.

For years, food had been imported into Mount Lebanon to supplement local agricultural production. Consequently, the disruption in food supplies by the Allied blockade was felt in some areas almost immediately. The time of year Turkey entered the war was also a factor. November coincided with the late harvest season. When men should have been in their fields and orchards harvesting crops in preparation for the approaching winter, they were conscripted in unprecedented numbers and put under arms. For the first time in Ottoman history, Christian men were drafted into the army. Demands for manpower were immense and went beyond filling military ranks. Some conscripts were assigned to laborer battalions to work on all sorts of civil engineering and military projects such as construction and maintenance of roads, bridges, and railways. Horses and other work animals were requisitioned, and in some areas trees began to disappear. Olive trees that provided one of the most basic foods in Mount Lebanon and Syria along with the majestic cedars were cut down and in the Beqa Valley mulberry trees were harvested by the Turks all to be used as fire wood to heat boilers in steam-powered locomotives that had been previously fueled by imported coal.[4]

Prices began to soar as the demand for food and other essentials exceeded available supplies. Adding to these woes was the near collapse of Turkish currency that took a dive and fed soaring inflation. While some might have hoped the worst was behind them, by the end of 1914, optimism vanished in the spring of 1915. At the same time the Allies were landing at Gallipoli, Mount Lebanon was struck by a disaster of apocalyptic magnitude: swarms of locusts. Nothing could stem their destruction, and, when the calamity ended, newly planted crops were gone, and trees were stripped of their bark. Economic havoc prevailed as prosperous businessmen and merchants in the commercial sector were financially ruined, but the most severe threat was to the people of Mount Lebanon who were faced with a crisis of widespread famine. As the disaster intensified, Turkish soldiers in search of food entered people's dwellings and seized whatever foodstuffs they found. Rations stored in preparation for winter were gone, and families had nothing to eat. Medical supplies, however meager, were also confiscated by the Turks.[5] The Ottoman administration supplied flour to a few select bakers in Mount Lebanon with orders that all production be delivered to the Turks. Compensation for this form of forced labor was often no more than a single loaf of flat bread per day for a baker and his family.[6]

The official Ottoman policy was egregious and prejudicial when food was available for distribution to the non-military sector of the Syrian population. In Damascus the Ottoman governor Ahmad Jamal Pasha prohibited the distribution of food to the Maronites in Mount Lebanon. The Maronite Patriarch, Elias Peter Hawayik, supported his community the best he could with the limited resources at his disposal, but his efforts were insufficient.[7] Established relief organizations in the US such as the Presbyterian Board of Foreign Missions and new groups including the Near East Relief, the Syria Mount Lebanon Relief Committee, the

Syrian Ladies' Aid Society of Boston, and the Syrian-American Relief Committee went into action. Some of the funds raised in the US were sent to Lebanon and Syria through the papal legation in Washington, DC and the neutral Spanish Embassy. The famine was by no means secret. As it intensified, Syrian-Americans sought support for their relief efforts from private citizens and government officials alike. Petitions from Syrian-Americans and a Congressional Resolution led President Woodrow Wilson on August 31, 1916, to proclaim "Saturday, October 21, and Sunday, October, 22, 1916, as joint days upon which the people of the United States may make such contributions as they feel disposed for the aid of the stricken Syrian people."[8] Over the course of the famine, several million dollars were raised, but American relief efforts could not stem the food shortage crisis.

Turkish soldiers cordoned off the Beqa Valley, thus eliminating food and other goods from entering Mount Lebanon from the east. Coupled with the Allied sea blockade in the west, the people of Mount Lebanon were caught in a deadly vice. With few options available, they took matters into their own hands to do whatever they could do to survive. In Zgharta, Badawi Simon's brother Sarkis and Sarkis's oldest son Boutros smuggled flour and other basic foods through Turkish lines.[9] Sarkis baked bread in his home for the local people. It was provided to everyone in Zgharta and, on at least one occasion, to a stranger who near death from starvation had staggered into the village.[10] When goat milk was available, Sarkis and Badawi's mother, Warda, made *lebne* and walked the five miles to Tripoli to sell or barter for food.[11] The children of Barbour Farchakh, one of Badawi Simon's cousins, desperate for money to buy flour, sold their land and olive trees little by little until they had no more to sell. Due to a lack of buyers, land could not be sold and converted into cash. This led to the contrivance of all sorts of exchange methods. By one account, there was a bartering arrangement that provided a means of exchanging olive trees for flour. It was based on a tree's circumference. If a man could reach around a tree it was worth a pound of flour. If it was large enough for two men to reach around, it was exchanged for five pounds of flour.[12]

Sarkis Naoum, a friend of Sarkis Farchakh, led young men and women at night into the Akkar region north of Zgharta where they would buy or barter black market food and smuggle it back to family and friends. One of the young women was Mareen Nakad who would in later years become the wife of Sarkis Farchakh's oldest son Boutros. Smuggling food in time of war and famine has always been dangerous and could sometimes lead to fatal consequences. This was the eventual fate of Sarkis Naoum who was killed under mysterious circumstances in 1917 near Mejdlaya on the road between Zgharta and Tripoli.[13]

When the Great War ended in 1918 and the Allied blockade was finally lifted, the number of deaths from famine and disease was placed at 100,000, one-fourth of the population of Mount Lebanon.[14] Other writers number the victims to have been as high as one-half the population. Unlike many other Lebanese and Syrian families the Farchakhs were fortunate; they had no dead relatives to grieve. Their survival was due largely to their ingenuity and perseverance and, as one observer noted, the grace of God.[15]

Syrian Americans Go to War

Early on the morning of March 9, 1916, a guerrilla force under the command of the Mexican Revolutionary General Francisco (Pancho) Villa attacked the small town of Columbus, New Mexico, situated about three miles north of the US- Mexican border. Villa's forces created mayhem, set fires, and shot anyone caught in the open. When the raid was over, much of Columbus lay in ruins, and at least seventeen Americans were dead.

The day after the raid, President Wilson announced a Punitive Expedition consisting of about 5,000 regular army troops under the command of Brigadier General John J. Pershing. An emergency spending bill was rushed through Congress authorizing recruitment of soldiers and raising the army to full wartime strength. Five days later on March 15, General Pershing and his troops moved out of Columbus and invaded Mexico.[1]

By March 24 the expedition forces were deep into northern Mexico but unable to find Villa. The army demanded more troops as friction between American forces and the Mexican government began to escalate. On May 9, the Texas, New Mexico, and Arizona National Guard units were pressed into service. The political situation continued to deteriorate when the Mexican State of Sonora, which shares a common border with Arizona, reportedly declared war against the US on June 19. The War Department, as it was known before Congress renamed it Department of Defense in 1947, was wired by the army with a call for 65,000 additional National Guardsmen to repel the threat of a Mexican invasion.[2]

While National Guard units were being federalized in the summer of 1916, Johnny Simon was living at home with his parents in Montgomery. On several occasions he had mentioned that he wanted to join the Alabama National Guard, but his parents, especially his mother, balked at the idea. Johnny was not yet twenty-one, the minimum age for enlistment in the Guard and the age requirement could not be waived without his mother's written consent. Shortly after his nineteenth birthday, September 13, 1916, he became insistent and threatened to leave home if his parents refused to meet with a National Guard Recruiter. They finally agreed to invite a recruiting officer to their home for discussion. He apparently allayed their anxieties because Catherine signed the consent form.[3] Johnny became a member of the Alabama National Guard on October 17, 1916 as a bugler and assigned to Headquarters Company 2nd Alabama Volunteer Infantry Regiment.[4]

The June 22, 1916 mobilization of National Guard units across the US to reinforce regular Army troops along the Mexican border had brought the Alabama National Guard into federal service. From June until October 1916 they had been in their home camps in Alabama waiting for transfer orders to the border. Johnny was barely sworn in when he and more than 5,000 Guardsmen comprising the 1st, 2nd, and 4th Alabama Volunteer Infantry Regiments were mustered at Montgomery's Vandiver Park. They were deployed to three sectors: San Antonio, Texas and Douglas, Arizona and Nogales, Arizona. At Nogales they relieved the California units who were transferred back home. Johnny's Regiment was stationed at Camp Little on the American side of Nogales which straddles the US-Mexico border. There was no fighting in the particular sector at the time and most of the Guard's work day was spent standing guard duty and training for various military activities.

By March 1917, a full year after the Columbus raid, Pancho Villa and his guerrillas were still at large. The US government decided to end the Punitive Expedition. All military personnel were pulled out of Mexico, victory was declared and the crisis subsided.[5] The Alabama National Guard was ordered back to Montgomery for demobilization.

Demobilization was underway across the US when on April 6, 1917 Congress declared war against Germany. The demobilization order was rescinded, and all units were kept on active duty. The Alabama National Guard was deployed throughout the State to guard government office buildings, transportation and utility infrastructures, harbors, waterways, and other important sites. These missions continued until August 5, 1917, when the Guard was again federalized and began to be organized and integrated into US Army units.

On May 18, 1917, six weeks after declaring war, Congress passed the Selective Service Act. It authorized the establishment of almost five thousand local draft boards to register and classify potential draftees. The first registration, slated for June 5, required men between the ages of twenty-one and thirty-one to register. Exemptions were granted to men with dependent families, those employed in indispensable jobs such as farming and defense plants, and men with physical handicaps.

Draft registrants fell into two broad headings: American citizens and immigrants. An American citizen might be either "natural born" or "naturalized." Immigrants fell into three categories: declarant, one who had declared his intention of becoming a US citizen; non-declarant, one who had not declared; and enemy aliens. This last group was comprised of men born in and still citizens of those countries that were part of the Central Powers. Syrians in the US were not classified as enemy aliens although they were from a province of the Ottoman Empire. This was due to the fact that the US, unlike Great Britain and France, never declared war against the Ottomans.[6]

Declarant immigrants were subject to the draft while non-declarant and enemy aliens were exempt. Both were permitted to volunteer for military service if they chose to do so. Among the thousands of Syrian-Americans who registered for the draft as declarants were Zaki Azar, Sam Barson, Mansour Leon, and Michael Zataney. Aziz registered as Sim B. Farshee and was listed as a "natural born" American, having been born in New Orleans. None of the declarants listed above claimed exemption of any kind although Zaki, Sam, and Mansour could have legitimately done so because they had dependent families.[7] Of these five men, Aziz and his cousin Michael Zataney served in the army: Aziz was drafted, Michael volunteered. Johnny Simon did not register because he was already a member of the armed forces. Nazha Hawie's son, Wadih, did not register because of his age.

One of the fundamental features of armed conflict is propaganda, and the Great War was no exception. The American public-at-large was not particularly enthralled with the idea of entering the European conflict, but after war was declared it became necessary to gain public support. On April 13 the Committee on Public Information was established by executive order. It was the official office of government propaganda that encouraged and legitimized a barrage of profundities from politicians, newspaper editors, popular songs, theatrical productions and the pulpit. Slogans such as "make the world safe for democracy," "end [German] militarism," and "the war to end all wars" were constantly repeated. Anyone reluctant to demonstrate their patriotism as a loyal American obedient to government edicts and pronouncements, be they conscientious objectors, German-Americans, draft dodgers, or immigrants were stigmatized as *slackers*.[8] In the larger US cities, slacker raids were conducted by self-appointed vigilante-patriots and government officials to round up men of draft-age who, in the opinion of the raiders, were not doing "their share." Some cases resulted in accused slackers being incarcerated. A few were lynched.[9]

The call for patriotism became the major tool for encouraging support for the war and suppressing anti-war sentiment. It was promoted with the creation of symbols of loyalty. The most potent was the uniform of a military service. Several organizations emerged to question men seen in public not wearing one. Some self-appointed patriotic organizations conducted their activities with the tacit approval of the federal government. One organization, the Knights of Liberty pursued German-Americans thought to be disloyal and who were on occasion subject to public floggings or being tarred and feathered. Another would-be patriotic group that emerged was the born-again Ku Klux Klan.[10]

There were rewards for those who demonstrated their patriotism to the satisfaction of the government and various patriotic groups. One of them was the acknowledgement shown families whose sons or husbands served in the military. The symbol for all to see was a pennant with a blue star usually placed in the front window of the soldier's home. When a soldier was killed the blue star was replaced with a gold one and from this movement was born the Gold Star Mothers.[11]

The first draft call came on September 5, 1917 but recruitment ads and speeches at war bond rallies encouraged young men to volunteer for military service and not to shirk their patriotic duty. Thousands volunteered before the first draft. One of them was Nazha Farshee Hawie's son Wadih who in 1917 was employed as a bookkeeper at Cudahy Packing Company in Birmingham. In April the zealously patriotic young man turned eighteen. Not wanting to be known as a slacker, he volunteered for the US Navy Reserve Flying Service known in the romanticized parlance of the Great War as the suicide squad. It was the name given to sailors who manned blimps as spotters over a battlefield or along seacoasts looking for submarines. Standing in a gondola suspended under a balloon, spotters had a bird's-eye view of a battlefield and, when deployed to coastal areas, could spot submarines under the ocean's surface. From their vantage points they radioed via wireless telegraph back to land-based artillery batteries or ships at sea to give the position of ground forces or enemy submarines. Defenseless eyes in the sky suspended from a tethered balloon providing crucial logistical and real time information to the Allies were tempting targets for German anti-aircraft guns and airplanes: hence the nickname suicide squad.[12]

When Wadih told his mother what he had done, she refused to have any part of it, slacker or no slacker. At the time he volunteered, the minimum age for military service was twenty-one and Wadih had only recently turned eighteen. Nazha proceeded to the recruiting office with documentation in hand and proved to the recruiting officer that Wadih was underage. The enlistment was cancelled, and he was unable to join the military without his mother's written consent which she refused to consider.[13]

The Selective Service Law was amended in August 1918, and the age parameters expanded to include men aged eighteen to forty-five. This made Wadih eligible for the draft. In deference to his mother's wish he did not volunteer for the Flying Service but did join the navy. On August 9, 1918, he reported to the Naval Training Station at Great Lakes, Illinois where he was stationed for the few remaining months of the war.[14]

Ashad G. Hawie was one of those Syrian immigrants who did not wait to be drafted. Like his cousin Faris Hawie before him, Ashad immigrated to the US from Swayr in Mount Lebanon. He was 24 years old when he arrived in 1914 and, during the next three years, established himself with an impressive record of achievements. Like many of his fellow Syrians, he started his life in the US as a route peddler. Within a relatively short period of time, he earned sufficient money to open a store of his own in Mississippi and later in Mobile. Along the way, he took time to travel across the US rallying Syrian-Americans and other citizens on behalf of the Syrian-American Relief Committee which he founded.[15]

Hawie had applied for US citizenship but had not completed the process when he volunteered for the 1st Regiment Alabama National Guard. He signed up after the unit had returned from the Mexican border to Vandiver Park in Montgomery which had been renamed Camp Sheridan. Guard infantry companies were encamped in tents throughout the fairgrounds waiting for incorporation into the AEF, the American Expeditionary Forces. Those companies comprising the Guard's 1st Regiment became the 167th Infantry Regiment of the 42nd Division, the renowned "Rainbow Division."[16]

General Pershing, now promoted to commander of the AEF, arrived in France with a small staff in June 1917. American soldiers, referred to as "doughboys," a term of uncertain origin, suffered their first casualties on the battlefields of France, September 4, 1917. Early the next month, Private Ashad Hawie was selected from a number of applicants and sent to France ahead of his unit for special training. The main body of the 167th did not arrive overseas until late November.[17]

When war was declared, Aziz was in Chicago attending the spring term at Jenner Medical College. When it ended, he remained in Chicago working as a clerk at Fair Department Store, the giant retail establishment located at State and Adams Streets. The first of three registrations for the draft was scheduled for June 5, 1917, and, on that day, Aziz registered with the Chicago draft board as Sim B. Farshee.[18] During the first draft call made on September 18, he was inducted into the army. He served for eighteen months in no less than five different organizations.[19]

His first station was Camp Jackson, South Carolina. He was assigned to the 117th and later the 320th field artillery batteries. Following a few weeks of basic training, he was transferred to Walter Reed Hospital in Washington, DC where he fashioned prosthetic limbs. As months passed and manpower requirements in Europe continued to increase Aziz was transferred again this time to the 41st and 43rd engineers. In September 1918, in preparation for deployment to France, he was ordered to Camp Gordon, Georgia.[20]

Aziz Farshee 1919

Even with the 1918 Selective Service's expanded age requirement, Sy Simon was seventeen years old and too young to register for the draft, but he was not too young to hold down a full time job. In 1917 and 1918, he lived in Mobile with his cousin Assad Leon and Assad's wife Saydeh working in an electric motor repair and rewind shop. The youngest Simon son, George, was not quite five years old when the US went to war and Badawi Simon was not physically fit for military service. The 1913 Montgomery County Board of Heath certification of his chronic rheumatism continued to be valid and as the Board stated he was "physically unable to do manual labor."

When the US entered the war, it brought about many changes in the national economy. At the local level towns and cities utilized their capabilities resulting in the expansion of their economies. With its heavy industries, Birmingham's economy grew with the production of war materiel and the port of Mobile became a major embarkation point. Montgomery was the site of Camp Sheridan which prepared men for transfer to France. It also became the leading city in Alabama for aviation training. The Wright Brothers had established the world's first civilian flight school there in 1910, and the facility known as Wright Field was used for military flight training during the Great War. In 1922 it was renamed Maxwell Field. The first air field constructed specifically for combat pilot training was Taylor Field out near the rural community of Pike Road. With the influx of soldiers to Camp Sheridan and aviation instructors and pilot trainees at Wright and Taylor fields, the economy of Montgomery entered a prosperous period.[21]

Political developments in Russia in late 1917 led to a series of events that were to have a direct affect on the Allies and AEF in France. The Russians were the eastern lynchpin of the Allies, and, regardless of their success or failure on the battlefield, they kept a number of German divisions tied down in the east and away from the Western Front. The 1917 revolution in Russia eventually led to the rise of a Bolshevik government that exploited the costs of the war. Russia had lost millions of men, the economy was in shambles, food shortages abounded, and the people were in revolt. On November 26, 1917, the revolutionary government headed by Vladimir Lenin unilaterally ordered the end of all hostilities against the Central Powers and Turkey. Peace terms were formalized in the March 3, 1918 Brest-Litovsk Treaty. With a million soldiers on the Eastern Front freed up for redeployment, Germany began transferring men and materiel to the Western Front in an attempt to defeat the allies, capture Paris, and win the war.

Meanwhile, in Alabama, Michael Zataney was continuing to establish himself as an optometrist. The first registration for the draft was slated for June 5, 1917, but he registered instead on June 1 during a business trip to Montgomery. On May 25, 1918, almost a year after registering and not being drafted, he enlisted in the army. He was sent to Bartlesville, Oklahoma for basic training as an army scout, but, once in France, he was assigned sniper duty.[22] When the few weeks of indoctrination in Oklahoma were completed, he returned to Birmingham on furlough. While at home to visit his mother, Katherine Shakra, and his sister Sara, he also spent time with Sally Sharbel, the young woman he hoped one day to marry.[23] While he was home, Doctor H.A. El-Kouri, a prominent Syrian physician in Birmingham and informal leader and spokesman for the Syrian community, congratulated Michael for volunteering for military service. During one of their conversations, Michael told him he had volunteered to serve his country, the US. A discussion ensued, and Doctor El-Kouri later quoted Michael as saying, "I want no greater glory than to die for the USA and the Allies. Turkey must be crushed, and the Syrians liberated."[24] As much as Doctor El-Kouri's recollection might sound somewhat contrived to portray Michael as a hero-patriot, Michael Zataney was quoted making similar remarks to Simon Klotz, the French Consul to Alabama and friend of the Birmingham Syrians.[25]

During his furlough, Michael, Katherine, and "Cousin Sarah" traveled to Montgomery to visit Michael's brother Sam Barson and other relatives and friends including the Simons. Frances Simon, nine years old at the time, recalled in later years sitting on Michael's knee as he told her stories about living in Zgharta as a child and being raised by her grandmother, Warda Farchakh. When he departed, he gave Frances a locket with his picture inside.[26]

Once his furlough was over, Michael traveled to Camp Sevier, South Carolina, where he became a member of the 321st Infantry Regiment of the 81st Division. On July 13, 1918, he began the circuitous thirty day trip to France where he arrived early on the morning of August 13. Beginning four days later and continuing until September 14, the 321st Regiment underwent intensive training to transform "men into soldiers." This was essential because, in the words of Corporal Clarence Walton Johnson author of *The History of the 321st Infantry*, most of the men were "raw recruits, some having less than two weeks training when they were sent overseas." The doughboys were told they would not be put into active combat lines but rather, stationed in trenches. The trip from the training area to their assigned sector on the Western Front was made by rail with soldiers riding in cattle cars and on open flat cars.[27]

By August 1918, US war production was in high gear. Tons of American war materiel filled a vital and urgent need for the Allies, but the commodity they needed most of all was men to fight the Germans. And men they got. The supply of doughboys increased exponentially in 1918; in March there were 85,000 in France and by late summer they were arriving at the rate of 50,000 per week until their numbers had swelled to 1.2 million by September. Across the US at all duty stations, non-combat military assignments were trimmed and every man who was physically fit was prepared for deployment to France. It was during this time that Aziz was caught up in the reassignment of personnel and in the process transferred from Walter Reed Hospital to Camp Gordon, Georgia.

Camp Gordon near Atlanta, Georgia was one of sixteen temporary camps constructed across the US under the war mobilization plan. At the time, it was the largest construction project in Atlanta history, covering 2,400 acres and designed to accommodate 46,612 men and 7,688 horses and mules. In addition to being a training facility, it was a staging site for troops about to be deployed to France. In the summer of 1918, Johnny Simon had been promoted to Sergeant Bugler, assigned to the 605th Engineers, and also transferred to Camp Gordon. Johnny the bugler and Aziz the optometrist-turned-prosthetics-maker were both assigned to transient companies at Camp Gordon by early fall.

In the summer of 1918 Badawi Simon traded in his car and purchased a new Model T Ford. That September, when he and Catherine learned that Aziz and Johnny were temporarily stationed at Camp Gordon, they drove the approximately 150 miles from Montgomery to Atlanta to visit them. When they arrived at the camp, they found that their sons were both confined to the camp stockade. A disagreement between the two brothers had erupted and led to fisticuffs, but they were nonetheless permitted to visit with their parents. Badawi and Catherine spent a day in and around Atlanta after visiting their sons and returned to Montgomery.[28] On October 11, Johnny was shipped to France.[29] When he arrived his unit disembarked and with little delay loaded onto railcars and transported non-stop to the Western Front. By this time the Meuse-

Argonne offensive was in full swing. Hundreds of Americans were being killed everyday and on some occasions musicians were utilized by the US Army Graves Registration Service to bury the dead. In addition to this grim duty, Johnny, now the Sergeant Bugler for his company, later recounted seeing the dark green waters of the Meuse River run red with blood. Meanwhile, in the US, Aziz was still at Camp Jackson, but, in early November, he and thousands of other doughboys were dispatched to troop transports destined for France.

Launched on September 26, 1918 the Meuse-Argonne offensive was designed to deliver the decisive death blow to German forces on the Western Front and bring the war to an end. At the time, it was the largest military operation of its kind in history. There were a million American doughboys facing the Germans. The intensity of fighting varied in different sectors and the one assigned to Private Michael Zataney's company had been relatively quiet.[30] This changed on October 9 when the Germans attacked. The Company's baptism of fire began with an artillery barrage of 3,000 to 4,000 shells. With fixed bayonets, the Germans came out of their trenches in two waves but the "green" soldiers of the 321st Infantry successfully repulsed the attack and suffered no casualties. A week later they were relieved by a French infantry unit and, on October 18, began ten days of intensive training in preparation for a new assignment. On November 1, the regiment was again loaded on trains and two days later arrived at Verdun where they took up their position about two miles north east of the historical fortress. Clarence Walton Johnson wrote that the destruction and desolation for miles around Verdun was so thorough that "nothing was left standing, not a tree nor even a bush." Without trees or foliage to cover their movements from sweeping German machine gun fire, the men of the 321st Infantry Regiment were exposed to constant mortal danger.[31]

On November 10 Private Zataney's company was at the edge of Moranville about six miles east of Verdun. Early the following morning, November 11, at 5:00 a.m. the armistice to end the Great War was signed in a railroad dining car in the Compiegne Forest near the French town of Rethondes. It was scheduled to take effect six hours later at 11:00 o'clock. During the six-hour interim the war raged on and the danger of being wounded or killed remained. One of those wounded on the morning of November 11 was Sergeant Ashad Hawie. Being injured in combat on the last day of the Great War in its closing hours was a curious twist of fate for a man who had arrived in France ahead of his unit, had been in France for thirteen months, and fought in all twenty-eight major engagements on the Western Front. He was seriously wounded on the outskirts of Sedan, but, after several weeks of convalescence, he recovered.[32]

As the dawn of November 11 broke over the Western Front, Aziz and several thousand doughboys were aboard crowded troop transports in mid-Atlantic. It was still dark when news of the armistice was received. With the fighting coming to an end and the AEF no longer in need of more troops, the convoy turned around in mid-ocean and returned to the US.[33] Within a few hours, it was common knowledge all along the Western Front that the armistice had been signed, and many American soldiers wondered why orders to attack German positions had not been cancelled. But, armistice or no armistice, all operational orders remained active.[34]

At 6:00 a.m., Michael Zataney's regiment was ordered to move out of its positions near Moranville and to advance to the east toward the village of Grimaucourt in a frontal attack against the Germans. By 7:30 a.m. the three battalions of the 321st Infantry Regiment had reached the area south of Grimaucourt. The German machinegun fire was incessant as the infantrymen trudged across an open marsh covered with heavy fog. For more than three hours, the 321ˢᵗ pressed forward and finally reached the German trenches at 11:00 a.m. Word was passed that the armistice was in effect, but the fighting did not come to an immediate halt. According to Brigade Commander Colonel George McIver, hand-to-hand combat continued for some minutes after 11:00 o'clock.[35] When the fighting finally stopped, the soldiers of the 321ˢᵗ Infantry looked up and down the German trenches and back toward the open ground of the "no-man's land" they had crossed. Between 6:00 a.m. and 11:00 a.m. nine soldiers of the 321ˢᵗ were killed and twenty-two wounded. One of the casualties was Michael Zataney mortally wounded at the close of the Great War. Along with other wounded soldiers, he was transported to the field hospital at Ancemont about ten miles southwest of Grimaucourt. He succumbed to his wounds either while in transit or at the hospital. Three days later, on November 14, he was buried at the Ancemont AEF Cemetery Number 548, one of the hundreds of temporary American military burial sites throughout France. [36]

News of his death did not reach his mother, Katherine Shakra, until November 27, the day before Thanksgiving. News did not travel as fast in 1918 as it does today. Additionally, the Meuse-Argonne offensive had gone on for almost seven weeks during which time 26,000 American doughboys, almost an average of 1,000 per day, were killed. Identifying the dead, preparing temporary burial sites, and the recording of information was time consuming. These delays resulted in some families not learning of their loved one's death for several weeks after the armistice went into effect.[37]

Michael A. Zataney 1918

When the notice of Michael Zataney's death appeared in the November 28 *Birmingham News,* shock rippled though the Syrian community at the loss of a well-known and respected young man. A memorial service was held on December 1, 1918 in the assembly hall at Saint Elias Maronite Church. It was attended by friends, relatives, and some Birmingham soldiers from the 321ˢᵗ Infantry Regiment. The main speaker was Simon Klotz the French Consul to Alabama who paid tribute to Private Zataney and all the Syrian-Americans who died in France.[38]

John Higham wrote "The government's official propaganda agency, the Committee on Public Information, made much of the decorations which individual immigrants received."[39] Among this group was Ashad Hawie, hailed in the US press as "a Syrian-American hero."[40] He had been awarded the Distinguished Service Cross by General Pershing and decorations for heroism by the governments of France, Belgium, Italy, and England. He was the most decorated soldier from Alabama and as far as can be determined the most highly decorated Syrian-American of the Great War. But he was not unique in his service to his adopted country. In his study of the conduct of US Syrians during the war Philip Hitti observed that among the foreign born, "the Syrians hold an enviable war record. In point of loyalty, patriotism and devotion to the institutions of this land, as demonstrated by war, they have been unexcelled --- even by the Americans themselves. Throughout the war when the US government compiled lists of pro-Germans and suspicious undesirable persons, 'not a Syrian name occurs.'"[41]

Citing a report by the Provost Marshal General and other War Department sources, Hitti continued: "no less than 13, 965 or about 7 percent of the whole Syrian [American] community served in the United States army." Syrian workers in defense-related industries were cited for their exemplary on-the-job performances, and, in the Second Federal Reserve District comprising New York and its environs, 4,800, Syrians "bought $1,207,900 worth of [war] bonds."[42]

When the parades ended and the brass bands fell silent, the glory of the moment subsided and all that was left was the grim business of burying the dead. During the war, the US government announced plans to temporarily bury in Europe all American soldiers killed there. The plan further stated that once the war was over the remains of those soldiers would be disinterred and returned to the US for permanent burial. Later, in an October 16, 1919 announcement, almost a year after the armistice and with all American soldiers killed in France still buried there in hundreds of temporary cemeteries, the War Department reaffirmed its policy but with modifications. The announcement stated that the remains of soldiers in Great Britain, Belgium and Italy would be returned to the US providing the nearest relative did not request an overseas burial. The policy for those temporarily buried in France, however, was the exact opposite. All fallen soldiers were to remain there for permanent burial unless the next-of-kin specifically requested the body be returned to the US. It is estimated that approximately 30,000 families decided to have their loved ones permanently buried in Europe. Katherine Shakra was one of the Gold Star Mothers who decided to have her son buried in France at one of the six cemeteries the US government planned to erect there. In addition to the French cemeteries, two others were planned, one each for England and Belgium.[43]

In 1923 Congress established the American Battle Monuments Commission. It was charged with overseeing the design of newly planned cemeteries including chapels and memorials. When the projects were completed in the late 1920s, the largest one was the Romagne Cemetery known today as the Meuse-Argonne American Cemetery near the town of Romagne-sous-Montfaucon.[44] Michael Zataney was moved from his temporary grave at Ancemont and became one of the more than 14,000 men buried there. Most of them died in the Meuse-Argonne offensive. On the gently sloping hill where the graves are carefully aligned Michael Zataney is buried in Plot D, Row 31, Grave 5. It is marked with a white Italian marble cross mounted in a buried concrete slab covered with well-manicured grass. The cross is engraved: *Michael A. Zataney, Pvt 321 Inf 81 Div, Alabama November, 11, 1918.*[45]

As early as 1920, private pilgrimages to Europe were made by mothers and widows to visit the graves of sons and husbands. Throughout the decade, public sentiment grew to send mothers and widows to Europe at government expense to visit the graves of their loved ones. Congress finally resolved several problematic issues, and legislation was enacted. Shortly before leaving office in 1929, President Calvin Coolidge signed into law a bill establishing government-paid pilgrimages to the eight US military cemeteries in Europe. They occurred between May 1, 1930 and October 31, 1933.[46] During that time, Katherine Shakra traveled to France with other Gold Star mothers and in the summer of 1931 visited her son's grave at the Meuse-Argonne American Cemetery.[47]

At the war's end, Katherine Shakra became a charter member of the American Legion Auxiliary at the Gorgas Post No. 1 in Birmingham. From 1918 until her death forty-three years later, she rode on the Gold Star Mother's float in the annual Armistice Day parade and later, after it was re-named Veterans Day.[48]

112 South Bainbridge

By 1919, after nearly ten years at 207 South Bainbridge, the Simon and Azar household had become too large for the house the two families lived in. The two younger Simon children, Frances and George, had, of course, never lived away from home but within a few months following the end of the Great War, the three oldest Simon sons were coming home. Aziz, Johnny, and Sy had not lived in Montgomery at the same time since the second half of 1916. In addition to the five Simon children, Mary and Zaki were now the parents to two young daughters, Catherine (Kitty) born in 1915 and Emma born in 1917, the Simon's first two grandchildren. But the Azars were about to add a new member as Mary was pregnant with her third child. The Simon house was simply too small, and the best alternative was to move to a larger home that could better accommodate two families.

In August 1919, Zaki acquired the large wood-frame house located at 112 South Bainbridge.[1] It had been the home of Zaki's brother George Azar since at least 1917.[2] Earlier in 1919, when Zaki bought the American Hat Company, it seems that he traded his financial interest in Hasson and Azar to George in exchange for the Bainbridge Street home.[3] The house sat in the middle of the short block north of the

Simon home and across the street from the site that in 1938 became the location of the Alabama Department of Archives and History Building. This three-storied, white-painted landmark sat perpendicular to the Azar home and faced Washington Avenue which separated the Archives building grounds from those of the state capitol complex. In 1949, the street address of the Azar house was renumbered to 116 South Bainbridge, but, for almost a year, 112 South Bainbridge was home to the Azar and Simon families. The one block move was made about three months before Zaki and Mary's first son, Joseph Azar, was born in October 1919.

The house covered most of the raised lot it sat on.[4] At the top of the ten steps that connected the house with the sidewalk was a comfortably sized open-air porch surrounded on its two open sides by a three foot high railing. To prevent toddlers and others from accidentally falling down the steps, a baby-gate was installed. There were several chairs placed near the railing and a swing was suspended from a metal A-frame. On hot days, a ceiling fan turned slowly overhead to circulate the air. At the time the house was purchased, the most popular social activity of the day was visiting friends and neighbors and engaging in conversation. The Azars' front porch was the place where a considerable amount of this kind of socializing took place.

Upon entering the house through French doors, there was a long hallway with a maroon linoleum floor below a crème-colored, twelve-foot ceiling that separated the rooms in such a manner that the house could be easily utilized as two separate apartments. It was an ideal arrangement. The living space was organized with the Simons occupying the rooms to the left, the Azars on the right. At the end of the hallway were two doors; the left one led to the kitchen, the right one to a bathroom. The kitchen was quite large, and, when traversed, it led to a modest-sized breakfast room. Adjacent to it and also behind the kitchen was the utility room. The house was home to the Azars and Simons until mid-July 1920 when the Simons moved into their own home about a block and a half away. But for the next four decades, the Azar home was the headquarters for social gatherings. Local relatives and friends stopped by for casual visits especially on Sunday afternoons and holidays or on special occasions like Christmas and Easter. Out of town visitors were often seen there: relatives and friends from Birmingham, Mobile, Troy, or other parts of Alabama. Other relatives came from Florida, Texas, and Arizona and sometimes visitors from the old country would be staying with the Azars. Dinner guests might include a priest or two or some nuns and occasionally Thomas J. Toolen, the Roman Catholic Bishop of Mobile.

In succeeding years as the extended family grew, Christmas became the grandest of occasions. Events that occurred during those long past decades spawned wondrous images that were etched for a lifetime into the memories of the adults and children who were there. For the season, a specially selected tree was purchased and decorated with all sorts of ornaments surrounded by colorfully wrapped presents sometimes piled a foot high or more. In some years, the tree was so tall that the silver star mounted at the top touched the living room's twelve foot ceiling. In a real Dickensian way there was always something for everyone, and Santa Claus and his merry helper never failed to show up to enliven the occasion and distribute gifts. Entertainment was provided by the Azar children and occasionally other extended family members in a variety of ensemble, duet, or solo presentations of musical selections, songs, magic acts, or other routines. As the number of Azar grandchildren and other youngsters came along, Zaki would sit in his chair on Christmas day with a sack of coins at his side. Children would line up and wait their turn to approach him and receive a coin or a gift, a wide smile, and a Christmas greeting. The joy of family and the happiness it brought added to the spirit of the season as cascades of laughter reverberated throughout the house.

Part of the Christmas season of those days included a number of guests staying in the house. There were times when there would be so many that attendance at Christmas Mass was made in shifts. The first shift went to midnight Mass and returned home to have a very early Christmas breakfast keeping the house in motion into the early hours of Christmas day. This freed up breakfast space for the next shift that attended Mass on Christmas morning. With dozens of people in the house, careful personnel management was required to ensure that everyone had a place to sit and enjoy Christmas breakfast. For Sunday lunch, not only on holidays or special occasions, it was not unusual for family members and guests to eat in shifts.

In Mary and Zaki's division of labor, Zaki was the bread winner. He worked every day of the week, including Sunday. After attending services at the Greek Orthodox Church of the Annunciation, he usually went to his store and worked until mid-day when he would go home for lunch and spend the afternoon with family and visitors.[5] Mary's role was more diverse. From the time she was four years old, she was surrounded by children. First, there were younger siblings followed later by her own children and then nieces, nephews, and grandchildren. She was fifteen years older than her sister Frances and eighteen years older than little brother George. Because of the age differences between Mary and her two younger siblings, she was in some ways their second mother. In addition to maintaining order and discipline within her own family, there were times when she was called upon to act as mediator between her siblings and their spouses in personal matters. Her day began with attendance at early Mass at nearby Saint Peter's, and her waking hours were filled with children and fulfilling family needs. Between her domestic chores, she managed to find time to visit with friends and relatives who dropped in.

Mary ran a well-organized and planned household. After attending an early Sunday Mass, she would drive downtown and pick up dozens of square rolls at the Electric Maid Bakery on Court Square. With these, she and the daughters would serve scrambled eggs, ham and sliced tomato sandwiches.[6] The Sunday noon meal often included kibbee, a universal favorite among Lebanese, stuffed squash (*qusa mihshi*), and stuffed cabbage (*mihshi malfuf*). Because of the number of people to feed on Sunday, preparation would often begin Saturday with squash being hollowed out for stuffing Sunday morning with ground meat, rice, tomato, onion and spices.[7]

Beside her routine daily activities, Mary also managed some private financial matters such as the money kept in a sort of slush fund. Zaki gave her the money from time to time, ear-marked for her brothers should the need arise. Few details of this practice are known, but it was part of the somewhat communal lives of immigrants. Private property was respected, and personal ownership was a clear-cut fact, but there was also the practice of looking after one another. The conditions for tapping the financial resources Mary controlled are not clear because it was not an openly discussed topic. Sometimes her funds were provided as a loan while at other times it was an outright gift.[8]

The Roaring Twenties

The social liberalization that was a hallmark of the 1920s did not cure the long-held prejudices directed toward minorities and immigrants. One canard that seemed to pop up from time to time was the question of whether Syrians were "white" or "Asian."[1] This was the litmus test that determined an immigrant's eligibility for naturalization. It had been answered by the courts in the previous decade, but the issue refused to die. Syrians were, indeed, indigenous to the Asian landmass but they were not "Asian" as the term applied to naturalization law which was intended to exclude Chinese and Japanese immigrants from US citizenship.[2] The courts ruled that Syrians belonged to a branch of the Caucasian race. Nonetheless, this finding did little to dissuade some politicians who choose to "play the race card" in their rhetoric and sloganeering. One such example occurred in 1920 when a political candidate in Birmingham named J.D. Goss ran for the office of Coroner. He advertised himself as "The White Man's Candidate" and circulated a printed bill which read

They [referring to local government] *have disqualified the negro, an American citizen, from voting in the white primary. The Greek and Syrian should also be disqualified. I DON'T WANT THEIR VOTE.*

If I can't be elected by the white man, I don't want the office [original capitalization].[3]

However, the prejudicial views of the boorish Mr. Goss, the Ku Klux Klan, and other such individuals and organizations did not represent a true picture of Syrian acceptance by American society. Scholars such as Alexa Naff overwhelmingly portray the relationship between Syrians and their "American" neighbors as cordial and friendly. Where prejudice existed, it was due to bias against foreigners in general, not Syrians in particular.[4]

Historians of the post-war period and the Roaring Twenties write that the US economy went into recession in the months following the November 11, 1918 Armistice. The downturn lingered and was one of the contributing factors that led to the Republican Party's 1920 victory that brought Warren G. Harding to the presidency. As do most economic conditions, the recession affected different areas of the country as well as individuals in different ways. Such was the case of Badawi Simon. On July 12, 1920, he purchased the house located at 723 Washington Avenue.[5]

It was the first home the Simons had lived in during their US years that was not a rental. Badawi purchased the home by paying $100.00 "and other valuable considerations" to a J.F. Morgan and his wife Mattie. One of the conditions of the sale was the assumption of a mortgage which carried a balance due of $1,600.00. It had been issued in 1911 by the United States Mortgage and Trust Company of New York in the amount of $2,500.00. Its terms and conditions included prescribed payment schedules that specified separate interest and principal installments. Everything was clearly spelled out: interest payments fell due on the first day of May and November of each year while the principal was reduced by annual payments of $100.00 that fell due on May 1 of each year.[6]

Based upon the terms of the Bill of Sale and the assumed mortgage instrument, there is good reason to conclude that Badawi Simon had made a sound business decision. The total amount of the mortgage in 1911 was $2,500.00. In the nine years between 1911 and 1920 the annual principal payments had been made on time for a total principal reduction of $900.00 leaving a balance due of $1,600.00, the amount Badawi Simon assumed. The $100.00 payment he made to the Morgans was more than likely to reimburse them for the principal payment they would have made two months earlier on May 1. In effect, Badawi Simon bought a home in 1920 for $1,600.00 ($17,500 in 2008 dollars) that had been valued at $2,500.00 nine years earlier.[7]

The Simon's new home was located on the north side of Washington Avenue, across the street from the Home Town Grocery. The neighborhood store has long since been demolished, and the place where it once stood is today dominated by the RSA Plaza. Years later, the Simon property gave way to the expansion of state office buildings. The corner of Ripley and Washington just east of the Home Town Grocery was the site of the nurses' dormitory for Saint Margaret's Hospital. It too is gone.

Doctor Simon's success as an optometrist helped him and his family move further down the path of the American dream and integrating into mainstream society. They owned an automobile and lived in a home of their own that was large enough to accommodate the entire family. The question of loyalty to their new country, a bone of contention for certain anti-immigrant groups, had been laid to rest after Aziz and Johnny had honorably served in the US Army. Their neighbors were of

Catherine Simon with Mary Simon Azar 1920

mixed ethnic heritages, and, as communicants of Saint Peter's Catholic Church, they mixed with "American" families. To complete the picture of a typical American family, eight-year-old George had acquired a white mutt named Champ.[8] Leisure time was always at a premium for Badawi, but his work routine gave him the opportunity to work half day on some Saturdays. On those occasions when he took off from work, he would often treat Frances and George to a matinee picture show. This was a certainty whenever a William S. Hart movie was showing; Badawi Simon and his two youngest children were ardent fans of the famed western star.[9]

In 1920, Aziz was working at the American Hat Company while Johnny pursued a career in music. Both were living at home, and, over supper one evening, Aziz and Johnny approached their father with an idea. Aziz had used Farshee as his surname since at least the time of his enrollment at Jenner Medical College in 1916. On the other hand, Johnny had served in the Great War as John Simon and in 1920 was still known by that name. Aziz and Johnny pointed out that their friends and acquaintances failed to understand why two brothers with the same parents who were both living and still married to each other had different last names. It was a confusing means of identification, and Aziz and Johnny wanted to simplify matters. They proposed to their father that the family drop the Simon surname and adopt en masse Farshee as the family name. Aziz and Johnny were young men in 1920, but their forty-seven year old father had a different perspective. Badawi Simon had transformed himself from peddler to licensed optometrist. He had pursued his new profession for at least five years and had integrated into mainstream American business life about as much as an immigrant could do in practical terms. He mixed with all segments of society, was a member of the Woodmen of the World fraternal organization, and, as he asserted, was professionally established as Doctor Bernard Simon. He was sympathetic to his sons' proposal and told them to use the new name if they wanted to, but he would remain Bernard Simon rather than go through a lengthy and unnecessary process of reinventing himself as Bernard Farshee.[10]

The outcome of the conversation led to Badawi's sons changing their surname from Simon to Farshee, although Aziz had only to continue what he had started some years earlier. Sy had not been party to the conversation, but he and Johnny talked later and decided that when each got married, they would do so using Farshee as their family name, not Simon.[11] Among the two girls, the question was a little different. Mary Simon had become Mary Azar in 1914 so the issue was irrelevant to her but not so with Frances. In 1920, the second and youngest Simon daughter was eleven years old and continued to be known as Frances Simon until she married John Miaoulis in 1929. The only known exception appeared when she was identified in her father's 1924 obituary as Frances Farshee. George was eight years old in 1920 and continued to be known as George Simon throughout the 1920s. His first known documented use of Farshee as his surname occurred in 1930 when the US Census taker listed him as George Farshee. At the same time, his mother was listed as Catherine Farshee, not Catherine Simon.

John B. Simon a.k.a. John B. Farshee

During his adolescent years, Johnny often found himself in trouble. By the time he was sixteen, he was hot headed, short tempered, and too quick with his fists.[1] During this time, he got himself into some kind of trouble and was remanded to the Alabama Boys Industrial School in Birmingham. Long after this event took place, two stories were told as to the reasons why it happened. Both could contain elements of the truth.

The first story alleged that Johnny was sent there by a judge as a juvenile delinquent, but years later when this story was investigated, no one could recall what his offense had been. The other story was that Badawi had exhausted his patience with him and was afraid he might take some action in a moment of anger that would cause irreparable damage in his relationship with his son. To get professional help, Badawi arranged for Johnny's admission to Alabama Boys Industrial School in Birmingham. This latter explanation makes a little more sense than the first because Johnny was taken to Birmingham by Badawi and Catherine, not by a law enforcement officer.[2]

Johnny Farshee 1921

Alabama Boys Industrial School was not operated by the state or governmental body nor was it structured like a reformatory, jail, or a prison. Rather, it was a facility conceived and founded by a civic-minded woman named Elizabeth Johnston. She wanted to establish a "school of opportunity" for young offenders. It was governed by a Board of Women, all mothers of boys who could give time to the school. Funding for Mrs. Johnston's project came from the Alabama State Legislature after she helped prepare and introduce the appropriate legislation. The school opened in 1899 and among Mrs. Johnston's rules was the prohibition of bars on windows and locks on dormitory doors. She refused to let the school have a prison atmosphere.[3] Johnny entered the school on January 12, 1913 and was there for two years. During that time there were no reports that he caused any trouble. When he finished his time at the school at age eighteen and returned home to Montgomery, he was a better adjusted and more sociably agreeable young man. Of equal or greater importance, he had become interested in music and learned to play various brass instruments including the bugle, trumpet, and trombone.[4]

After his stint in the army during the Great War, Johnny returned to the US from France in the summer of 1919. The next year he was on his way to becoming a professional musician. But in his case the term musician went beyond being a sergeant-bugler in the army. There were all sorts of musicians dedicated to performing a broad mixture of musical forms in a number of styles and in a variety of musical organizations. To understand the kind of musician Johnny was and the talent he developed, one must look back to the last decade of the nineteenth century.

Beginning in the late 1890s and continuing until the advent of the Great Depression, there were two major musical movements in the

US that more or less paralleled each other. The first was the birth of ragtime, the immediate precursor of jazz. It was a synthesis of minstrel songs and African-American dance rhythms often mixed with elements of European music by composers such as Frederic Chopin and Johann Strauss. The other movement began with the arrival of the concert band, usually consisting of brass, woodwind, and percussion instruments. This was Johnny's calling. His interest was in performing with brass bands and ensembles that played marches, overtures, and classical compositions arranged for bands and instrumental solos sometime requiring virtuoso proficiency.

As ragtime increased in popularity, so did marching and concert bands. Band leaders often enjoyed popularity comparable to today's pop stars. There were a number of them, but among the most well known were bandmaster-composers Karl King, Henry Fillmore, and John Philip Sousa. Their compositions were inspired by popular social, patriotic, and political themes of the day or commissioned by institutions such as newspapers or most any enterprise that wanted a march written and named in its honor. A popular Sunday afternoon form of outdoor family entertainment was a concert in the park.

Between 1893 and 1903, John Philip Sousa's Band featured a trombone soloist named Arthur Pryor. He was considered by critics and aficionados as the world's greatest trombonist.[5] One story told about him occurred during a European tour of Sousa's band. It seems that after a concert in Germany where Pryor performed some of his flashy and highly technical solos, his trombone was taken on the sly by some students who wanted to examine it. They were convinced that a gadget or something was embedded in his horn that allowed Pryor to perform in a manner few had imagined much less heard. The horn, once examined, was found to be no different from any other and was returned to Pryor.

Johnny was inspired by Arthur Pryor's trombone mastery, and he emulated Pryor's style. Arrangements of traditional tunes such as "The Blue Bells of Scotland," "Oh, Dem Golden Slippers," and "The Carnival of Venice" were basic in the virtuoso repertoires of the day and musically arranged in a somewhat formulaic manner. The tempo of the opening or exposition was slow and the melody easily recognizable. It was followed by one or more variations on the original theme and ended with a version that required an inordinate degree of technical proficiency. In some arrangements, the last variation was written in such a way that a listener would hear a melody line and accompaniment emanating simultaneously from a single trumpet or trombone. Johnny had the talent and ability to perform in this manner.[6]

Bands came in several varieties. Some were community, volunteer, or service organization bands, and some were professional. Others were strictly concert bands or marching bands, and, for circuses, there were bands that played all sorts of music. Some of the compositions and arrangements performed by circus bands were technically demanding, and this was where Johnny found his first full-time job as a performing musician. During the winter of 1920-21, circuses operated by Jerry Mugivan and Bert Bowers made Montgomery their winter home. A chair in the trombone section became vacant, and Johnny auditioned for it. He was hired. With the arrival of springtime 1921, the circus was pulling up stakes for its annual road tour. Johnny had a job and a new future and decided the time was right to get married.[7]

In 1921, there were several families in Montgomery named Moses. Some were English, some Jewish, some African-American. There were also two Moses families who were Syrian-Americans. One was Mike and Mary Moses who had immigrated to the US in 1890. They settled in Montgomery, and Mike established himself in the restaurant business.

Within a year, Mary Moses gave birth to their first child, a daughter named Monzora who in 1908, at age sixteen, married Katherine Shakra's oldest son, nineteen year old Sam Barson. The young couple lived with her parents' on King Street a block or so from the state capitol building. Mike Moses' brother and sister-in-law Paul and Eva followed Mike and Mary to Montgomery when they immigrated in 1894. Paul supported his family working as a carpenter. Over the course of their marriage, he and Eva were parents to seven children: two boys and five girls. The one who became part of the Simon-Farshee family story was their oldest daughter Dora.[8]

Johnny and Dora had known each other for years, and, on April 4, 1921 they were married at Saint Peter's Catholic Church in Montgomery. The marriage certificate identified him as John Farshee, not John Simon. To live in a more centralized location for Johnny's circus job, they relocated from Montgomery to Canton, Ohio. Canton, the hometown of President William McKinley, is often associated with the Pro Football Hall of Fame established there in 1963, but, during the decade of the 1920s, it was quite a show town with several top-rated theatres and a sure stop for traveling shows and performers. It was a thriving community that included a number of Syrians and, according to some, known as "Little Chicago" because of the bootleggers and gangsters who lived there. Among the well-known celebrities who had performed in Canton was the renowned Italian tenor, Enrico Caruso, who sang in concert during his 1919 US tour. Many other well-known personalities filled Canton theatre bills over the years and in October 1921, the ever-popular Sousa Band was scheduled for several performances.

Early in their marriage, Dora became pregnant with her first child. She often traveled with Johnny as the circus took him throughout the Midwest but in August with her advancing pregnancy Johnny reduced his time on the road. When they were not traveling, the young couple's home was an apartment at 427 Market Avenue South in Canton. Johnny enjoyed plenty of work and, for a time, was associated with Karl King, "The March King," who lived in Canton around this time. Johnny arranged and transcribed some of King's compositions. He also performed with local pit orchestras that accompanied vaudeville shows and silent movies. Oftentimes, Dora went to the circus or the theatre with Johnny when he performed in the orchestra.[9] This seemingly safe and innocuous activity turned out to have fatal consequences.

The name of the town where Dora was injured has apparently been lost. A search of the *Canton Registry*, the only Canton newspaper available today on microfilm, makes no mention of the incident in any of its editions published between late August and early September 1921. Obituaries published in the Canton and Montgomery newspapers were brief and offered no details associated with the circumstances surrounding Dora's death. An investigation by the Stark County, Ohio District Library Genealogical Section turned up nothing and the medical records of Aultman Hospital where she died only go back to 1979. In the absence of documented details, the account that emerges is based upon family oral history and information obtained from Dora's detailed death certificate.[10]

Working with dates and entries on the death certificate, Doctor Sara DeHart of Lynnwood, Washington, associate professor Emeritus of Nursing, the University of Minnesota, developed a timeline of events leading to Dora's death. According to Doctor DeHart, the timeline probably began sometime between forty-eight and seventy-two hours prior to September 7, 1921, four days before Dora sought medical help.[11] As the story has been told, she was attending a circus with Johnny who was working in the band. One of the acts staged featured a bull. While the performance was underway, the animal suddenly leaped into the audience for some unknown reason. It ran rampant and, during the melee, "brushed" against Dora. After it was restrained and the incident subsided, it seemed that no one including Dora was seriously hurt.[12] Doctor DeHart hypothesizes that within a day or two Dora began to complain of acute mid-back pain and parts of her body began to swell. When these symptoms appeared, Johnny immediately sought the best medical treatment available. He took her to the Fraunfelter Clinic at 435 Market Avenue South in Canton a few houses from his and Dora's apartment.

The Fraunfelters, father James and son Clare, were extraordinary physicians in their day. When Canton's Aultman Hospital, Stark County Ohio's first hospital opened in 1892, James Fraunfelter performed the first surgical procedure in the new facility. His medical training was extensive. It included course work at the Cincinnati College of Medicine and Surgery and Long Island College Hospital in New York where he graduated in 1871. The next year he enrolled at the Jefferson Medical College of Philadelphia from which he also graduated. Later he took a post-graduate course at the College of Physicians and Surgeons in New York. Following graduation from that institution he moved to Canton and established his practice. His son Clare was equally well educated. They put their medical education into a practice that specialized in the surgical treatment of women's diseases in a time when medical specialization was a rarity and a physician's practice devoted to women's diseases almost unheard of.[13]

On the morning of September 11, 1921, Johnny and Dora arrived at the Fraunfelter Clinic. She was examined by Clare Fraunfelter who determined that the unborn fetus was still alive but Dora was seriously ill suffering from nephritis, an inflammation and infection of the kidneys. Following his examination, he had her checked into Aultman Hospital.[14] As her condition turned critical, Doctor Fraunfelter explained to Johnny the seriousness of the infections and its possible consequences. According to what Johnny later told his sisters and others he got on his knees and begged Doctor Fraunfelter to abort the fetus in an attempt to save Dora's life.[15] But a procedure of this kind was not available. The therapeutic abortion of a living fetus was not an option in 1921, not even to save a mother's life. A procedure of this kind was not declared legal until the US Supreme Court issued its landmark decision in the 1973 Roe v. Wade case. Had Doctor Fraunfelter performed the abortion Johnny begged for, he not only stood the risk of losing his medical license he would have been subject to criminal prosecution by the state of Ohio.

Two days later, September 13, when the fetal heartbeat was no longer detectable, Doctor Fraunfelter surgically removed the dead fetus. But the nephritis remained and became progressively worse. The state of medicines and other necessary procedures and equipment were about the same in 1921 as they had been when Johnny's uncle Rumanos underwent a nephrectomy a decade earlier. The medical options available to Clare Fraunfelter were too limited and there was nothing he could do to treat the deadly and advancing nephritis. Dora's condition continued to deteriorate. Johnny remained at her bedside throughout the ordeal and was there when she died at 5:00 a.m. Saturday, September 17.

An autopsy was not performed, but Doctor Fraunfelter filled out the death certificate in detail. He stated that the cause of death was "premature birth [with] acute nephritis." A separate entry read "pregnancy with nephritis [duration] ten days" (the brackets are Doctor Fraunfelter's). Her age was recorded as twenty-two years, ten months and twenty-five days.[16]

Dora's body was taken from Aultman Hospital to C.A. Spiker Funeral Home on Tuscarawas Street in Canton and prepared for burial. That evening she lay in state from 7:00 p.m. until 9:00 p.m. Shortly after nine o'clock, her casket was transported to the railroad station for the 10:00 p.m. departure for Montgomery.[17] Johnny, with the casket of his dead wife, left Canton that night and arrived in Montgomery the next day, Sunday. On Tuesday, September 20, following a Requiem Mass at Saint Peter's, Dora Moses Farshee was buried at Oakwood Cemetery. Johnny and Dora's life together lasted one hundred and sixty-six days, a little more than five months. The day after she was buried was Johnny's twenty-fourth birthday.

Johnny stayed in Montgomery for only a short time and returned to Canton to continue his career and rebuild his shattered life. Music gave him solace. He eventually took a job as a music teacher with the Canton public schools and during that time arranged and composed music for circus bands. Among his original compositions was a trio of works titled *Smearin' Trombone No. 1*, *Smearin' Trombone No. 2*, and *Smearin' Trombone No. 3*. Each was similar in style with the band playing various melodies or accompaniments to trombone glissandos or "smears." A smear occurs when a trombonist sustains a note and extends or retracts the instrument's slide. One of the styles of circus music where trombone smears were utilized was known as "walk about" music written specifically as an accompaniment to the antics clowns performed between regular acts.[18] Johnny never earned much if any royalty from his compositions, and he did not renew any of the copyrights. But his music survived. Over eighty years after *Smearin Trombone No.2* was composed, it is today recognized as a circus band classic and can be heard on certain CD collections of circus music.

In 1931, his Canton years came to an end and he returned to Montgomery. The effects of the Great Depression had shut down most of the entertainment facilities where he had earned his living, but technological developments also contributed to the changing times. Circuses and live theatrical performances were giving way to radio and motion pictures. The golden era of the great marching bands and traveling circuses had come to an end. He operated a music store on the second floor of the building that housed the American Hat Company and became band director at Montgomery's Lanier high school (later Baldwin Junior High School). He subsequently remarried for a second time, a widow named Bessie Sullivan from Pine Level, a rural community south of Montgomery.

***

A few months before the death of Dora Farshee, Rumanos made one of the major decisions of his life. He and his family would return to Lebanon, a newly created country that did not exist in history as a territorially and politically defined nation-state before 1920. That year the French governing Syria and Lebanon under what was to be legitimized as a League of Nations mandate detached Mount Lebanon from Syria and annexed to it the coastal cities and lands extending from the Kebir River in the north, south through Tripoli, Beirut, Sidon, Tyre and onto Naqura on the Israel–Palestine border. To this new territorial arrangement, they annexed the Beqa Valley, the lush agricultural plain that bordered Mount Lebanon on the east. Because the new state included areas not originally part of nineteenth century Mount Lebanon, the French High Commissioner for Syria, General Henri Gouraud, gave the new 4000 square mile country the name *Grand Liban*, Greater Lebanon. Certain Lebanese living abroad saw the emergence of a Lebanese state as a dream come true and an opportunity to return home with their newly acquired wealth.

By the time the Great War ended, Rumanos was on his way to accumulating sufficient money to finance moving himself and his family from Detroit, Michigan to Lebanon. Among the possessions he planned to take to the old country was an Oldsmobile.[19] In addition to the luxury of having a car in Lebanon, Rumanos planned to establish a taxi service between Tripoli and Zgharta, a distance of about five miles.[20] After getting the necessary travel documents in order, Rumanos, Susie, their four children, and the Oldsmobile departed New York on May 21, 1921.[21] Details of the trip are not available, but their arrival in Zgharta must have been quite impressive. Rumanos, who had immigrated in 1903 as a teenager with "empty pockets," had returned eighteen years later with a Syrian-American wife and English-speaking children all dressed in the latest Western fashions and riding in an American-manufactured automobile.

The wealth Rumanos returned to Lebanon with contrasted sharply with that of his brother Sarkis. In 1921 Sarkis and his oldest son Boutros were working for the French mandatory government at El Ruins, located in Syria between Baniyas and Tartus. They were stonecutters engaged in road construction. Sarkis's son, Tannous, the youngest son by his first wife, Latifi Mjelli, was a gendarme employed by the French mandatory authorities. Rumanos started his taxi service between Zgharta and Tripoli, said to have been the first of its kind in North Lebanon. It was unsuccessful, but it was not his only endeavor.[22] He hired several villagers from Zgharta including a young man named Maroun Brahim who helped cultivate Farchakh land.[23]

Alabama - the Early 1920s

Major events within the US family in 1921 included Rumanos's return to Lebanon and the tragic death of Dora Farshee. The following year, 1922 the Simon's fourth grandchild, Margaret Azar was born. During the next year, 1923, two more Simon grandsons were born: Edward Azar and the first child of Sy and Addie Forshee, Joe.

At the end of the Great War, Sy returned from Mobile to Montgomery and took a job as an electrician at the World War I army air corps training site that eventually became Maxwell Air Force Base. For several years, the Simons had been neighbors to a family named Smith who had a strikingly attractive daughter named Addie. She had known the Simons since childhood. Sy had been enamored with her for years, and, on January 27, 1922, the young couple eloped and drove the forty-odd miles to Selma, Alabama to get married. It was here that Joe Simon officially became Sy Forshee. He was baptized Joseph and, in his youth and early adult life, was sometimes known as Joe Simon. Among friends and family he was "Sy," short for his traditional Arabic name Said, which means happy. His surname change from Simon to Forshee, not Farshee, was the result of uncertainty over the spelling of the adopted family name. While in Selma, Sy telephoned Aziz in Montgomery.

The telephone connection was faulty and Sy misunderstood what his brother told him. He was married using the name Forshee rather than Farshee. When the spelling error was discovered, Sy considered returning to Selma and having the record corrected but he kept putting it off. Following the birth of his and Addie's first child, Sy decided to leave the spelling as it was.[1]

Because they had eloped without telling Sy's parents of their plans, Sy and Addie returned to Montgomery and kept their marriage a secret. She lived with her parents and Sy continued living with his. When the announcement appeared in the Selma paper, Sy took a copy and gave the clipping to his father. Badawi Simon chided Sy a little but was happy for him. The problem was that Sy did not want to be the one to tell his mother he had eloped, so Badawi volunteered to give her the newspaper announcement at a time he deemed appropriate. When Catherine was told about the marriage, she was upset for a while, but she soon accepted the fact that Sy had married a young woman she had known for years.[2]

To improve his economic status, Sy and Addie moved to New Orleans where Sy took a job as a maintenance electrician in a hotel. The young couple lived there for about a year. In 1923 their first child, Joe, was born. The job did not work out and in late 1923 Sy, Addie, and Joe returned to Montgomery. They lived with Badawi and Catherine while Sy searched for a job. He read a want ad in a newspaper for an electrician's job in Jacksonville, Florida and wrote the prospective employer. After some brief negotiations, he was hired, and, during the week before Easter 1924, Sy and his family moved to Jacksonville where he and Addie remained for the rest of their years.[3]

Sy Forshee 1921

Within weeks of Sy and Addie's move to Jacksonville, the annual principal payment came due on the Simon home. The final payment was made a few days before the May 1st 1924 due date when Badawi paid off the remaining balance of the mortgage. A handwritten note at the bottom of the first page of the mortgage document confirmed that the terms of the mortgage had been "Satisfied in full."[4]

Johnny and Sy no longer lived in Montgomery. With the additional free space in the Simon home, Badawi went about converting the single family dwelling into two separate apartments. He hired Kahlil Shakra and his brother Assad to do the remodeling. The Shakra brothers lived in Birmingham, but, being self-employed peddlers, they rearranged their route schedules in such a way that it allowed them to spend part of several weeks including weekends in Montgomery to work on the renovation.[5] By mid-November, except for a few minor details, the work was about finished. It had been an ambitious project. A number of walls were moved and new ones constructed along with the installation of a second kitchen and bathroom. The original floor plan had a hall that ran through the center of the house from the front porch to the back door. When the rooms were divided to form the two apartments the hall remained on the Simon's side and existing doors leading off the hall into the newly created apartment were walled up. The large parlor on the front of the Simon side was cut in half by a new wall, and the newly created front room became Aziz's bedroom. The room behind the new wall was a large bedroom with a double bed for Badawi and Catherine and single beds for Frances and George. The bathroom was behind the master bedroom. The last room was a newly built kitchen the Shakras constructed after enclosing the back porch.[6]

Across the hall, the new apartment had basically the same layout except there was no hallway, and the bathroom was in the back of the house next to the kitchen. When all the work was finished, 723 Washington remained the Simons' address, and the new apartment was numbered 725 Washington.

It was mid-afternoon on Friday, November 14, 1924, when Catherine returned home from her visit with the Azars. She wanted to be there when Frances and George came home from school. At about 5:45 p.m. the telephone rang. The caller was Joe Money. Catherine listened silently for a few moments and hung up the phone. She began to sob and told Frances and George that "Papa" was dead. With her children in hand and all three in a state of near hysteria, she walked over to the Azar home and told Mary what had happened. After overcoming her initial shock, Mary telephoned the Dexter Avenue Y.M.C.A. where Zaki often played volleyball on Friday evenings and told him what had happened. He rushed home and telephoned Assad Barad who within minutes arrived at the Azar home. A short time later, an ambulance picked up the two men, and they proceeded to Dublin. After Badawi's body was transferred to the ambulance, they headed back to Montgomery. Zaki rode in the ambulance, and Assad followed in Badawi's car. In about an hour, they reached McCarthy-Spruell Funeral Home where Zaki made the funeral arrangements.[7]

Sy and Addie drove up from Jacksonville and arrived late Saturday evening. Johnny came in by train from Canton the next morning. The requiem Mass and burial had been scheduled for Monday but was postponed until Tuesday. It had taken all day Saturday to locate Badawi's sister Nazha, and the extra day was needed for her to travel to Montgomery. On Monday, the casket was moved from the mortuary to the Azar home because the Simon house remained in the final stages of renovation and could not be readied quickly enough to accommodate the casket and dozens of visitors. Zaki and Mary's living room and the adjoining dining room were better suited.[8]

After the casket arrived and flowers were arranged, relatives and friends entered the room to view the body and begin the all night wake. Some quietly wept, some talked in hushed tones, others prayed. Time passed and suddenly a curious noise began to be heard in the distance causing those who took notice to turn to each other with questioning looks on their faces. It was the sound of funeral mourners.[9]

No one recalled who hired or invited them. Family members who remembered those sad November days said the wailings and lamentations of the half-dozen or so men and women were heard inside the house while they were still out on Bainbridge Street. As they came up the stairs and filed into the house a crescendo of crying, shouting and screaming grew into a nerve-jarring cacophony.

They surrounded the open coffin and kissed Badawi Simon's forehead as all family members had done and then their performance began. They spoke to the body as if it were alive asking it to say hello to the other family members and friends who had died earlier. Some fell across the casket as they wailed, others dropped to the floor crying. They reminded those present of what a good man Badawi Simon had been and made connections between him and other dead members of the Syrian community. While some told that his wife was a loving spouse and devoted mother others wailed "what is his poor widow to do" and "what will happen to those two young children with no father?" Some of the mourners were almost out of control in their portrayal of grief and when those family members and friends who were not already in tears began to cry, the mourners filed out of the house went back down the stairs onto Bainbridge Street and were gone. To them the tears they helped conjure up were a demonstration of how much Badawi Simon was loved. The outpouring of grief was a final tribute to him. Many of those who saw all this, including some of Badawi Simon's children, had never seen such a spectacle. The two youngest, twelve-year-old George and fourteen-year-old Frances were frightened by the funeral mourners, and they thought they had come to steal their father's body.[10]

Those unfamiliar with the ways of the Orient might find this story bizarre. But the practice of mourning the death of a loved one in the manner demonstrated by the funeral mourners is a tradition that goes back in Middle East history to at least the time of the ancient Sumerians. According to archeologist Joanne Farchakh-Bajjaly chronicles of death and mourning recorded across the ages reveal that little has changed over the course of centuries.[11]

The scene at the Azar home on November 17, 1924 was one of the cultural accoutrements that came to the New World with Syrian immigrants. Nonetheless, tradition or not, Montgomery, Alabama was not the Middle East, and the performance of the funeral mourners was not appreciated. Badawi Simon's sudden and unexpected death was sufficient in itself to cause grief without the gratuitous theatrics of outsiders. The incident proved so unsettling it was decided that evening to never allow outside mourners to be part of a family funeral.[12]

The following morning, Tuesday, November 18, services were held at Saint Peter's followed by the burial in Oakwood Cemetery. His flat grave stone reads "B. Simon Farshee – August 16, 1872 – November 14, 1924. The 1872 date is probably erroneous. According to his father's journal Badawi was born in 1873. Below the date of his death are words written in Arabic script. They translate as *Badawi Semaan Farchakh, Ehden Lebanon.*

Badawi Simon had a life insurance policy with Woodmen of the World that paid Catherine eight hundred dollars which in 2008 would have been equivalent to a little over $9,800.00. How the money was spent is not known but there was no such thing as burial insurance in 1924, and some of the money no doubt went toward paying burial expenses. The renovation of the Simon home was all but completed but money was still owed for building materials and whatever remained due to the Shakra brothers.[13]

Adjusting to the loss of Badawi Simon's income was the next hurdle faced by the family. Unlike Selma Leon who could step into Mansour's shoes and operate his business, Catherine did not own a store and was not trained in any profession or trade. The first thing to be done was to shore up her finances which Aziz, Johnny, and Sy agreed to do. The afternoon of the funeral they agreed that each would provide their mother with a prescribed amount of money on a monthly basis.[14] But they were not the only ones to step in to fill the void. In the years following the death of Badawi Simon, it was not unusual for Zaki Azar to drop by the Simon home for a short visit with Catherine. They were on the best of terms, and each enjoyed occasionally pulling pranks on the other. One time he sneaked into the coal bin behind the house with the idea of making a sudden appearance in the kitchen. Catherine, not knowing who it was, heard a noise and went after the imagined intruder with a kitchen knife. Fortunately for Zaki, she discovered who it was before attacking.[15] According to Frances and George, when Zaki visited their home, he would invariably walk into the kitchen all the time chatting with Catherine and casually look into the pantry. The next day a grocery truck would arrive with foods to restock the shelves.

As time passed, the family tried to come to terms with their loss, but Catherine was inconsolable. She donned the traditional black garments and went into mourning. Frances and George recalled coming home from school to often find her crying. She would sometimes sit and listen to Arabic language phonograph records, and one particular song she played lamented being away from Ehden.[16] Her grief over the loss of her husband continued for the rest of her life.

Tragedy, Orlando, a Marriage and Another Emigration

The sorrow over the death of Badawi Simon had diminished little when New Year 1925 arrived six weeks later. But among the grief and sadness, there was at least one glow of happiness when Sy and Addie Forshee's first daughter, Catherine, was born in February. But whatever reprieve from grief her birth might have brought it proved to be temporary. Around the time of Catherine's birth, two of the Azar children, Joseph and Margaret, became ill. What had begun with a cold and coughs turned into pneumonia.[1] Margaret survived the ordeal, but Joseph was not as fortunate. After a few weeks of being treated at home, he was admitted to Saint Margaret's Hospital on March 25. The progress of the infection could not be stopped, and his condition continued to deteriorate until the early afternoon of April 1, 1925 when he died.[2]

Badawi Simon's sudden death in November, barely five months earlier, had been an enormous shock and source of grief, but the death of Joseph Azar was not the same kind of loss. When Badawi died, the male life expectancy in the US was about fifty-four, and at age fifty-two most of his life was behind him. But Joseph was a five-and-one-half year old child, and part of the tragedy of his death was his entire life was in front of him.

The death of her father followed by the death of her son less than five months later had a crushing effect on Mary. She was a strongly family-oriented person and very close to her father. She had lived in the same house with her parents from the time she was born until the Simons bought their own home in 1920. The closeness of family was part of her makeup and on occasions she is said to have commented that she wished the family all lived in close proximity to each other like families did in the old country.[3] Within ninety days of Joseph's death, Mary, who was six months pregnant when he died, gave birth to daughter Dodie (Josephine). The effect of these cumulative events occurring within a relatively short period of time was beyond her endurance. Her emotional condition continued to be problematic, and Zaki came to the conclusion that the only way he could help his wife would be to get her away from Montgomery.[4] That said, the problems associated with getting away from bad memories and temporarily moving from Montgomery involved much more than packing up the children, getting in the car, and hitting the road. Several crucial arrangements had to be made which Zaki proceeded to do.

The first question was where they should go and how Zaki would earn a living. Then there were the questions of what would be done with the home on Bainbridge Street, and what about the American Hat Company? Talking with friends in the Greek community, Zaki and an acquaintance named Steve Maradis, an immigrant from the isle of Patmos who had been in Montgomery about a year, decided to go to Orlando, Florida and operate a restaurant.[5] Zaki was not a restaurateur in the strictest sense of the word, but he had owned the Lunch Box Restaurant a few years earlier. The home on Bainbridge was rented out, and Aziz was entrusted with the management of the American Hat Company. To reduce Mary's domestic load, the two oldest children, Kitty ten and Emma eight, were boarded at Loretta Academy. On Friday afternoons they went to Catherine Simon's home for a weekend with their grandmother, their aunt Frances and uncles Aziz and George.[6] When all these arrangements were finalized, Zaki and Mary loaded their car, and, with their three youngest children, Margaret, Edward and Dodie, set out for the almost five-hundred mile trip to Orlando.

At the time it seemed that Orlando was the place to be because it offered Zaki and his partner Steve Maradis an opportunity to take advantage of the Florida boom. With the addition of another Greek immigrant, George Sostis, Zaki and his partners took over the operation of a business named Eddie's Restaurant. Established in 1923 by two brothers, Eddie and Tony Langiotti, it was advertised as "The Home of Real Pastry." Eddie became the sole owner in 1924, and for the next year the business flourished in its original location on Church Street in downtown Orlando. In 1925 Eddie moved it into the ground floor of the Hotel Empire.[7]

The Empire was located on Central Avenue in the center of downtown. With its "One Hundred Rooms, Electric Elevator, Steam Heat, Hot and Cold Running Water, Etc., Phone in every room, open all year round, European Plan," it was among Orlando's leading hotels. During the time they were in Orlando and Zaki's involvement in Eddie's Restaurant, he and Mary and their three children lived in the Empire. The advertised rate was one dollar per room per day.[8]

From what Zaki and his partners knew about Florida, the venture was expected to be financially rewarding. In the atmosphere of economic prosperity across much of the US, the Sunshine State had emerged as the place to go for families to vacation and for others to retire. An economic boom was underway in the early 1920s fed by tourism, new construction, and land speculation. The enthusiasm for Florida began to waver after an unusually cold winter in 1925 that was followed by an extremely hot summer in 1926. Natural disasters including hurricanes and floods added to the state's woes and the economy nose-dived. By the middle of the decade just as Mary and Zaki were getting to Orlando, the Florida Boom was giving way to the Florida Depression. The natural disasters and bad weather of 1925 and 1926 had an adverse affect on Eddie's Restaurant as it did on other businesses.[9] After about a year, Zaki, Mary and the children returned to Montgomery. The amount of Zaki's financial loss during the months spent in Orlando is not known but it is said that the venture was quite costly for him.[10] With his departure another Greek immigrant, Lucas Gazes, took his place in the operation of Eddie's Restaurant. As the decade continued a state of normalcy returned and so did the birth of children. Zaki Azar Junior and Dot Forshee were born in 1927, and, in 1929, Helen became the newest member of the Azar family.[11]

Aziz, in his management of the American Hat Company, had not been confronted with the economic troubles that plagued Zaki's restaurant venture in Orlando. In fact, while the Azars were away, business had been very good, and the store had grown significantly. An expanding business needs additional employees, and, in 1926, Aziz hired an attractive young woman originally from Rockford, Alabama named Mary Artie Bates. He had originally met her when she worked as a clerk at one of the variety stores on Dexter Avenue. Not too long after Artie, as she was known to all, went to work at the American Hat Company, it became apparent that the relationship between she and Aziz was more than just employee and employer. Following Zaki and Mary's return to Montgomery and toward the end of 1926, Aziz and Artie were married. He was thirty-two, she nineteen. After their marriage, they lived in the Simon home with Catherine, Frances, and George.[12] Their son Billy was born in 1928. Three years later, they became parents again, this time to twin girls, Mary Catherine and Emma Frances.

Meanwhile, in Lebanon, Rumanos might have imagined a tranquil life in his native land utilizing the knowledge and job experiences acquired in the US. But, he too was confronted with realities that had a long term affect on him and his family. In the 1920s the notion of Lebanon as an established unified state was more of a political idea than a national reality. Not all its citizens favored the Maronite-driven quest for a state independent of Syria, especially the Greek Orthodox and Sunni Muslim populations of Tripoli. Political sentiment in this North Lebanon city, the country's second largest, favored remaining a part of Syria. Additionally, the unilateral French decision to sever the Beqa Valley from Syria became a source of discord between the Mandatory authorities in Beirut and the Syrian government in Damascus. Aside from political wrangling, there were violent conflicts from time to time between certain groups and the French Mandatory authorities. When the League of Nations assigned the Mandate for Lebanon to the French it had not met with popular acceptance among all nationalist groups. Among them were the Druze who responded to various French undertakings by openly revolting in 1926. Two rebel groups, each totaling more than one thousand men, attacked French positions and convoys. Roads and railroads were cut as well as telephone and telegraph lines. Skirmishes erupted between Druze and Maronites in the Beqa Valley and the Jabal Akroun northeast of Tripoli.[13] Scores of Christian villages were sacked, and fields under cultivation were burned. Several hundred Christians were killed or wounded, and commerce in and out of Beirut halted. Thousands were affected. Many fled North Lebanon and the Beqa and went to Beirut.[14]

Rumanos probably never anticipated these political upheavals. How they might have contributed to his decision to leave Lebanon a second time is not known. Maroun Brahim said in a 1982 interview that Rumanos's decision to leave Lebanon happened without warning, and the disposal of the land and his car was done in great haste.[15] The Oldsmobile was not sold by the time he left Lebanon. To sell it and act in his behalf, he assigned power of attorney to a man named Jamil Hage. Hage was supposed to sell the Oldsmobile, collect the proceeds, and forward it to Rumanos.[16]

Rumanos and his family immigrated to Brazil in December 1926. They attempted to return to the US but were denied entry because of immigration restrictions imposed by Congress.[17] Although he had lived in the US for eighteen years, Rumanos had never become a citizen. The fact that four of his and Susie's children were born in the US meant nothing to US immigration authorities. From their perspective, Rumanos and his family were little more than another group of "Syrians" seeking entry into the US at a time when immigration laws permitted only one hundred Syrians per year to do so.[18]

George Simon's Mobile Years

Sometime in late 1926, increasing tension emerged within the Simon household. The problem swirled around the relationship between Aziz and George. There were nineteen years' difference in their ages, and certain generational and personality dissimilarities brought the two brothers into frequent conflict. Problems had been ongoing but they seemed to worsen after their father died. George was twelve at the time, and several men of good heart including family friend Sam Hadden tried to fill the void. He would often take the youngster fishing, a form of recreation George enjoyed throughout his adult life. Aziz and Zaki did what they could to help with the disagreeable youngster but with little success.[1]

Part of the problem was Catherine's protective nature as it applied to all her children but especially to "her baby." When Badawi died, she told Aziz that he should take his father's place as the head of the family. But, as it turned out, that didn't work with George, and, in her own subtle way, Frances too rejected the idea. Even before his father died, George had acquired the habit of throwing temper tantrums when he did not get his way. Sometimes he would beat his head against a wall or get on this hands and knees and literally pound his forehead on the floor. This juvenile silliness became the source of his nickname, Buster, which was originally *head-buster.*[2] In response to these antics, Catherine said little if anything. When George had an altercation with a neighborhood playmate, he would run to his mother who would immediately call on the playmate's parents and read them the riot act. Being typical children, the boys would soon be at play again, the disagreement forgotten, but in the process of protecting "her baby," Catherine created hard feelings with some of her neighbors.[3]

Among some of young George's other unsettling acts was the habit of running up and down the hall shouting repeatedly at the top of his lungs for no apparent good reason "murder, fire, police…murder, fire, police." Frances and Sy said it was unsettling and could occur at any time of day. No one—including Aziz—could discipline him without Catherine's interference.[4]

With all this said, George's behavior was not caused entirely by Catherine's pampering. When Badawi was living and returned home from a few days' business trip, he usually brought small gifts for Frances and George. To some degree, less than Catherine, he too pampered George probably because the Simons came from a culture noted for indulging their children especially boys.[5]

Yet, the predicament between Aziz and George was in some ways quite complex and went well beyond the problems associated with parental pampering or sibling rivalry. They were about as different as two people could be. Aziz, like his sisters Mary and Frances, had the temperament of their father which was more serene than the temperaments of Johnny, Sy, and George which favored their mother.[6] There were other significant differences. Being nineteen years older than George, Aziz had lived the history of the family. He was the first born and as a child had traveled to Lebanon and back with his parents. When he was growing up with young parents who were still in the process of learning to converse in English, he spoke Arabic. George understood little of this complex tongue and had gone through none of the experiences Aziz had shared with his parents.

Summed up, Aziz was an even-tempered man with a multi-faceted personality, diverse interests, and broad experiences. He was a no-nonsense person who had little tolerance for childish impudence. On the other hand, George had no firsthand knowledge of his parents' earlier struggles but had been born after many of their trials and errors had been played out. As 1927 arrived, the conflict grew more intense, and other problems with the youngster were emerging. At Saint Peter's Boys School, George's academic and behavioral performance was marginal. As these problems accumulated, a decision was made that was somewhat akin to what Badawi Simon had done with Johnny in 1913.[7]

Aziz and Zaki agreed that George needed to be in an environment where he was subjected to better discipline, and the only way to accomplish this was to get him away from home. When they first mentioned the idea to Catherine, she flatly refused. Discussion continued over a protracted period, and, after considerable haggling, she was finally talked into accepting the notion. In August 1927 fifteen-year-old George Simon went to Mobile where he was enrolled at the Boys' Industrial School. This was the same institution where his cousins George, Michael, and William Leon had been enrolled following the death of their father, Mansour. George's arrival at the school coincided with major changes that were underway in the institution's structure.[8]

The director, Brother George, was focused on developing a curriculum for the boys to be trained and prepared for some trade. As his program was being set up, Thomas J. Toolen was consecrated Bishop of Mobile on May 4, 1927. These two men collaborated in their efforts to gather the necessary resources and laid the plans for school workshops to be constructed for teaching metal and electrical work, pipe fitting, and shoe repair. The classroom curricula included courses in mechanical drawing, design, and other trade-related subjects. With the support of local businesses and community artisans, apprentice programs were organized that allowed students to utilize their school training in real jobs or in any trade a student wished to pursue.[9] George Leon, Mansour's oldest son, took advantage of the program and became a printer's apprentice.[10] Brother George went a step further and formed a Working Boy's Club. He monitored the personal habits of those who held off-site jobs and encouraged thrift with their income. He required that they open a savings account and provide him with a full accounting of their expenditures.[11]

The school's expansion projects promoted by Brother George and Bishop Toolen had been underway for about three months when George Simon arrived for the 1927 fall term. What he encountered was probably different from anything he had been exposed to. Brother George maintained a disciplined environment and encouraged serious study, and George Simon seems to have fallen into step with relative ease. Some of his interests were apparently inspired by his older brothers, Johnny and Sy. He joined the band under the leadership of Brother Florien and learned to play the baritone horn, trombone, and tuba. For his trade education, he studied electrical theory and application with the intention of becoming an electrician as Sy had done over a decade earlier.[12] In some of the photographs dating from this period, George is seen posing next to electrically wired demonstration boards that were built for an electrical course. Another photograph from this period appeared in the April 14, 1929 edition of *The New York Times*. It shows baseball legend Babe Ruth posing with the school band holding George's tuba. The New York Yankees baseball team was in Mobile for an exhibition game, and the Boy's Industrial School band provided music for the occasion. Before the game began, "the Babe" was asked to pose with the band and hold the instrument he played when he was enrolled as a youngster in a Catholic boy's orphanage in Baltimore.[13]

George Simon remained with the Brothers of the Sacred Heart through the spring semester of 1929. Frances and his mother visited him regularly during his two-year stay. Sometime Mary and her older daughters accompanied them. Traveling to Mobile afforded Catherine the opportunity to visit relatives and long-time friends. When George left the Brothers in the summer of 1929, he went to Jacksonville and lived with Sy and Addie. During that time, he worked in Sy's electric motor repair shop.[14] Around Christmas, he returned to Montgomery and put his education to work by taking a job as an electrician's helper in the maintenance department at Montgomery Fair Department Store.[15]

Another reason George returned home when he did was because his mother would soon need him as a companion and helper. Frances had been at Catherine's side in the years following Badawi's death. She was a quiet person who had grown up in the shadow of her older sister, Mary. But she was quite industrious. The same year George went to Mobile, she graduated high school and took a job as a cashier at the American Hat Company to help support her mother. While working there, she met John Miaoulis, a friend of Zaki Azar. On April 20, 1929, they married and moved into a rented apartment on Mildred Street.

The Great Depression and
Catherine Simon's Last Years

With the advent of the Great Depression, the Farshees, Forshees and Azars faced the most difficult economic time any of them encountered during their years in the US. True, Badawi and Catherine had been in the US in the 1890s when the country suffered an earlier depression but this one was worse. Measured by unemployment, loss of income, duration or any other statistical index, the Great Depression of the 1930s was more devastating than the one of the 1890s.[1]

As the economic situation worsened, Zaki Azar assumed more and more responsibility. In addition to helping provide for Catherine Simon and others, his own family continued to grow since the "Crash of '29" with the births of George (1930), Tommy (1933), Dottie (1934) and Jimmy (1936). Undaunted in his determination to help all those he could, he became the family employer of last resort.[2] If someone was out of work and no job could be found, he or she worked at the American Hat Company. Zaki was under considerable financial strain, but he kept his store afloat by careful management of the money it brought in and borrowing against his life insurance policies.[3] His reputation as an astute businessman kept him on good terms with the First National

Bank of Montgomery where business loans were available to him.[4] He paid his vendors according to agreed terms, and they were always ready to extend him credit.

The economic distress of the Great Depression was not the only source of grief for the family. There had been no major tragedies within the extended Montgomery family since the death of Joseph Azar in 1925, but tragedy struck again in 1934. That year whooping cough was going around among the children of Aziz and Artie. During a coughing spasm, one of the twin girls, Emma Frances, was unable to expel the mucous that had caught in her throat. In desperation, Artie sent for a neighbor, Irene May, a nurse at nearby St. Margaret's Hospital, who was a lodger at the Barnett home next door. Ms. May was unable to help the child, and she choked to death. Baby Frances, as she was known, died February 22, 1934 four days after her third birthday.[5]

Later that year an ongoing dispute that was at least ten years old came to life again. Toward the end of December Catherine received a letter from Brazil. The return address read Romao Simao, the Portuguese equivalent to Roman Simon, that is, Rumanos Farchakh. In recounting this event years later, Frances, who was with her mother at the time, said their first thought when they saw the letter was that Rumanos had finally acceded to Catherine's request for her share of the proceeds from the sale of family land in Lebanon.[6]

When Catherine opened the envelope and pulled out the contents she held a four inch by six inch photograph. There was no money or bank draft. On the back of the picture written in Arabic was a single sentence that read "To the wife of our brother in memoriam." The date under the salutation was a few days after the tenth anniversary of Badawi

In Memoriam 1934

Simon's death. Pictured in the photograph were four men: Youssef Semaan Farchakh and Rumanos, seated, both brothers of Badawi Simon plus Youssef's second son, Bakkos and Boulos Farchakh one of the younger brothers of Boutros Sarkis Farchakh . As Catherine stared at the picture she began to cry. Rather than offer any consolation on the tenth anniversary of her husband's death the picture opened old wounds and reignited a long standing grievance.[7]

Rumanos's 1921 return to Lebanon is one part of a larger story. The other part told by the US family began when Badawi Simon was still living. It had to do with the sale of the Farchakh land in Lebanon and the distribution of the proceeds. The story endured for decades after Badawi and Catherine were gone and it continued to be told and retold as long as any of the Simon children were living. Today it is remembered by some of the Simon grandchildren and is known among members of the old country family.

Prior to Rumanos's departure from the US he and Badawi had discussed the sale of Badawi's share of the family land. Rumanos was expected to return to Lebanon and act on his brother's behalf.[8] After Rumanos arrived in Lebanon and about two years passed Badawi heard nothing. He became disconcerted to such a degree that he talked about traveling to Lebanon to determine what was going on but died before making the trip.[9] When the land issue remained unresolved and Rumanos sent no money the story grew ever larger and what emerged within the Simon family was a story that was a combination of facts, myth and invective.

To unravel this story the Simon version is recounted first and followed by the facts that were subsequently uncovered.[10] In the Simon version Rumanos was living in Brazil in 1924 at the time of Badawi's death.

When he decided to leave Lebanon after his return there in 1921 and made the decision to emigrate once again he had wanted to return to the US but had been refused entry because of newly enacted Congressional legislation.[11] Rather than remain in Lebanon and unable to enter the US, Rumanos and his family went to Brazil where his older brother Youssef had been living since 1906. Now living in Brazil, and upon hearing of Badawi's death, Rumanos traveled from Brazil to Montgomery where he met with Catherine. George Farshee, George Simon at the time, said he came home from school one afternoon and upon entering the house saw Rumanos talking with Catherine. According to George's account made years later he was convinced the man was Rumanos because of the physical similarity the man bore to his father, Badawi Simon. During that meeting, Rumanos prevailed upon Catherine to give him power of attorney so he could sell the Lebanon property. The understanding between the two was said to have been that Rumanos would travel to Lebanon, sell the property and send Catherine her share of the proceeds. With Catherine's power of attorney in hand Rumanos left Montgomery, departed the US for Lebanon, sold the Farchakh property and returned to Brazil.

Months passed and Catherine heard nothing. She dictated several letters to Frances and mailed them to Rumanos in Brazil asking for her share of the proceeds. He did not ignore her inquiries but answered that there was no money to send "because there wasn't any."[12] In the absence of any further explanation the story assumed its own dynamic. The acrimonious legend that evolved told of Rumanos coming from Brazil to Montgomery where he hoodwinked Catherine into giving him power of attorney at the time she was grieving over the death of her husband. He left Montgomery, traveled to Lebanon, sold the property, pocketed the money, went back to Brazil and refused to send Catherine her share.[13]

Without indicting or acquitting Rumanos of any real or imagined unsavory conduct this story was found to be fraught with improbabilities and inaccuracies. First of all, Rumanos was not in Brazil in 1924. He was in Lebanon according to old country sources and the first hand testimony of Maroun Brahim.[14] Between the time Rumanos returned to Lebanon and Badawi Simon died the only substantive news that reached Montgomery announced the death of Sarkis's son Tannous in 1922. Compounding this loss was the death of Sarkis a short time later having grieved himself to death.[15] Rumanos did not emigrant from Lebanon to Brazil until 1926 and, in fact, he never entered the US after he and his family departed New York in 1921. His sister Nazha and he were very close and the familial affection between brother and sister extended to her son Wadih Hawie who held Rumanos in high esteem. When asked during a 1981 interview about his uncle returning to the US in 1924 or 1925 or at anytime after his return to Lebanon, Wadih stated unequivocally he never heard of any such visit and further stated that it would not have occurred without Rumanos seeing Wadih's mother, Nazha. Wadih added that Rumanos had planned to travel to the US after World War II to visit Nazha and other relatives but she died before he made the trip and it was subsequently cancelled.[16] The claim that Rumanos was seen talking to Catherine a few months after Badawi's death was explained as a case of mistaken identity. According the Sy Forshee, the man young George Simon saw talking with his mother was probably a family friend, Boutros Makary whose physical appearance, Sy stated, was somewhat similar to that of Rumanos and Badawi.[17]

In 1982 Maroun Brahim was a semi-retired businessman living in Puebla, Mexico. When interviewed that year he said that one day in the mid-1920s Rumanos suddenly began the process of getting his family packed to leave Lebanon. Maroun stated that in preparation for his departure Rumanos "sold everything."[18] When the investigation of Rumanos's activities was extended to interviews conducted in Lebanon it was confirmed that he was eager to leave the old country. It was also said that a man with power of attorney named Jamil Hage, sold the Oldsmobile after Rumanos departed Lebanon but Rumanos did not receive any of the money.[19]

Determining what happened to the land remained unanswered until July 2004. During a conversation in Ehden the author learned that the original document for the sale of the land had been discovered in a box of old papers in Angele Farchakh's home in Zgharta. They had belonged to her father-in-law Boutros Sarkis Farchakh and after his 1985 death the unopened box was stored in her attic. While going through the contents a few months prior to the 2004 Ehden conversation, Angele discovered the bill of sale.[20] It was dated November 8, 1926. Rumanos had sold the land to his nephew Boutros Sarkis Farchakh, the oldest son of Sarkis Semaan Farchakh. Syrian currency was the medium of exchange but the amount paid is not given. Whatever Catherine Simon's share might have been she never saw any of it. Today the property is owned by Boutros's descendants and the land that caused much grief to Catherine Simon is a large orange grove.[21]

As much as Catherine might have wanted the dispute with Rumanos settled to her satisfaction there were other issues at home that affected her life. In 1935 she again became a grandmother when Frances and husband John Miaoulis became new parents to their only child, a baby girl, Mary Virginia. Later the same year the Miaoulis family moved into their new home on Madison Avenue.[22] Catherine enjoyed visiting her children and in the summer of 1935 she and her ten-year-old granddaughter Dodie Azar traveled by train from Montgomery to Jacksonville to visit Sy and Addie.[23] The Jacksonville grandchildren were now four in number with the 1931 birth of William Forshee.

All the Simon children were married by this time except George but that changed in October 1936 when he married Helen Boone from Dothan, Alabama. After their marriage, George moved out of his mother's home on Washington Avenue and he and Helen rented an apartment in Riverside Heights. George's new bride had graduated from nurse's training at Saint Margaret's Hospital in Montgomery and, following a year of post-graduate study at Johns-Hopkins Medical Center in Baltimore, returned to Montgomery and worked at Saint Margaret's as a registered nurse.[24] To help the newlyweds achieve a sound financial track, Zaki Azar was instrumental in George securing a job in the planning section of the Alabama State Highway Department.[25]

By 1937 the Depression was still plaguing the country and its destructive force was increasing in intensity in Montgomery. Money was tight and income from paying boarders for single rooms at 723-725 Washington was not available.[26] Although Badawi Simon had paid off the mortgage six months before his death the property was apparently later used for collateral on a loan. No public records were discovered to indicate whether the loan was for the 1924 remodel of the Simon home or some later purpose. Nonetheless by mid-1937 payments fell behind and there was no viable option but to surrender the house to the lien holder.[27] No record of foreclosure was discovered in the Montgomery County records office but whatever the financial circumstances were the property was lost.

George Farshee 1936

Catherine was invited to live with the Azar or Miaoulis families.[28] If she had wanted to she could have moved to Jacksonville and lived with Sy and Addie and their family but this would have taken her away from Montgomery where, with the exception of Sy and his family, all her children and grandchildren lived.[29] However, by 1937 it was said that Catherine had decided she was a burden to her children. Rather than live with either of her daughters or move to Jacksonville to live with Sy and Addie a small apartment was rented for her in September 1937 at 6 South Ripley Street.[30]

It was said that she enjoyed her apartment which was easier to maintain that her larger home had been. She was not isolated nor did she live as a recluse. Friends and relatives often stopped by to visit with her, usually unannounced, and on some occasions away they would all go for an outing. Aziz, Mary, Johnny, Frances and George who all lived in Montgomery maintained daily contact with her. Sy wrote to her at least once a month and sent money when he could.[31]

In May 1938 George Farshee's wife, Helen, confirmed that she was pregnant with their first child. After seeing the doctor the expecting couple went to Catherine's apartment to tell her the news. When first told of the pregnancy Catherine was delighted but after a while she turned somber. She and Helen were in the kitchen preparing supper and during their conversation Catherine told Helen she would "not live to see her baby's baby." Helen, not knowing of any particular illness her mother-in-law had assured Catherine that she would, indeed, live to see the expected child.[32] As events unfolded over succeeding months it became evident that Catherine knew more than Helen realized.

During that time Catherine began to loose weight and by the summer of 1938 her weight loss became noticeable. She was never a large woman and when she was considered to be in the best of health her weight was barely more than one-hundred pounds. When asked how she was feeling she answered that she had no appetite.[33] Her daughters encouraged her to see a physician which she initially refused to do but on July 30 she finally gave in and was examined by Doctor Fred Williamson. He diagnosed her condition as arterial sclerotic heart disease; in laymen's terms hardening of the arteries. What treatment he might have prescribed is not known. Her health continued to deteriorate and in late November Doctor Williamson diagnosed a second ailment, acute bacterial endocarditis, inflammation of the lining of the heart membrane.[34] A symptom of this malady is that one or both heart valves do not close tightly and therefore leak. Doctor Williamson would have detected this by hearing abnormal valvular sounds. She was hospitalized and seemed to her visitors to be in reasonably good spirits but continued to eat less and less food. The acute bacterial endocarditis rapidly progressed and its symptoms of fever and cardiac pain persisted. There was little Doctor Williamson could do; no antibiotics had been developed to effectively treat the bacterial infection and artificial heart valves were unheard of. The end came during the afternoon of December 27, 1938.[35]

The day after she died her obituary appeared in the *Montgomery Advertiser* under the bold print heading of *Mrs. Catherine Farshee*.[36] In the text she was referred to as Catherine *Simon* Farshee but a number of her friends did not attend her wake or funeral service or even know of her death until some days later. They recalled seeing the obituary heading but said the name Farshee meant nothing to them because they knew her only as Catherine Simon.[37] In addition to the obituary heading there were other sources of confusion about Catherine Simon. The engraving on her flat gravestone which lies next to her husband's in Oakwood Cemetery is not consistent with certain known facts.

It reads *K*atherine *C*oury, wife of B. Simon Farshee August 17, 1877 – December 28, 1938. The date of her death was December 27, not December 28. Her death certificate reads that she was sixty-four years old which would have placed her year of birth in 1874 and is consistent with other records.[38] On her son George's birth certificate her maiden name is spelled Koury, not Coury and her given name was more often spelled Catherine rather than Katherine.

Her prophetic statement that she would not live to see her "baby's baby" turned out to be true. Louis Farshee, George and Helen's son, was born twenty-two days after her death. Their second child and the last Simon grandchild, Catherine Jane Farshee, was born in 1941. All totaled she was a grandmother to twenty-two children of which twenty grew to adulthood. These grandchildren eventually became parents to over fifty children and from them and their children the descendants of Badawi and Catherine Simon now number in the hundreds.

The Way of the Emigrants:
For Better or Worse

During the Simon family's return to Lebanon in 1897-1899, Badawi had been willing to do the almost unimaginable when he went against his father's wishes and made a second emigration. Catherine's wishes cannot be stated with any degree of certainty, but there is circumstantial evidence that she probably would have preferred that they all remain in the old country. Yet, they came back to the US which had been in the throes of an economic depression for all the years of their first immigration. In addition to the economic factors, starting a new life thousands of miles away from homeland and family was more than a move from a traditional society. By comparison to the lifestyles they left behind, the move to the US was a genuine cultural shock. The growing American republic was unlike anything the Simons would have seen in Lebanon. It might be said that perhaps the one noticeable similarity between the US and the old country was the humidity in South Alabama which is comparable to the weather in some of the lower elevations of Lebanon. Each is equally uncomfortable in the summer. But regardless of the hardships and negative aspects of the New World, the US at its worst was better than Mount Lebanon with the stagnation that prevailed under four centuries of Ottoman domination.

Catherine's immigrant experience, when viewed separate from her husband's, is unique to her. When she and Badawi married, she was sixteen years old. Shortly thereafter, they left Mount Lebanon in search of a new life in the New World. Some of what they found in New Orleans and Mobile could not have been anticipated. There were times when the Gulf Coast was the target of tornadoes and hurricanes, illness and death from outbreaks of yellow fever epidemics not to mention election riots, random lynching of African-Americans and other minorities, and political malfeasance. She worked with her husband during his early peddling years and saw first-hand the physical strain of his work. In 1893 when they found themselves penniless and stranded in Tampa-Saint Petersburg, the question must have crossed her mind asking if immigration to a new land regardless of its promises was worth all the grief, hardship, and disappointment.

Nonetheless, Catherine persevered during the first immigration. She grew older in years, and one might speculate that during that period she "grew up." When they all returned to Lebanon in 1897, she was twenty-four years old. She had first-hand experience with life in the US, had given birth to two children, and had another on the way. When Badawi made the decision to return to the US, it is doubtful that his father would have told him to emigrate alone and leave Catherine and the children with him in Lebanon had he not had Catherine's acquiescence. Badawi's decision might have been as unsettling to her as it was to his parents, but under no circumstances would she have stayed in Lebanon and agreed to her husband returning to the US without her.

The death of Badawi Simon brought to an end a marriage that endured for over thirty years. It also severed Catherine's closest link to the old country, and, with his death, it was time to go into mourning. The traditional period was one year. While in mourning, a widow dresses in black and avoids festive occasions and events. When November 1925 rolled around, and the year of mourning was up, her daughter Frances said it was all she and her sister Mary could do to get their mother to stop wearing black or at least add a colored blouse or sweater. By 1938, notwithstanding the fact that she suffered from a serious cardiac condition, Sy and Frances said she evidently reached a point where she imagined she was a burden to others and, still grieving over the loss of her husband, decided it was time to die. She survived her husband by thirteen years, thirteen months, thirteen days.

Badawi Simon never fulfilled his ambition of funding an orphanage, and whether he would have accumulated the resources to do so will never be known. But as fate would have it, his youngest son George was enrolled in one, the Boys' Industrial School in Mobile. But funding an orphanage was only one ambition that brought the bold young couple to the US. Badawi and Catherine's emigration was driven by the desire to build a new life for themselves and their children as fully assimilated Americans. In this respect, they were successful. *Abu Aziz* and *Umm Aziz*, born into the peasant class of Mount Lebanon, Syria, became Doctor and Mrs. Bernard Simon, middle-class American citizens of Montgomery, Alabama. As adults, none of the Simon children traveled to Lebanon, nor did they express any interest in living there. The social and religious traditions under which Badawi and Catherine grew up were supplanted by their children and descendants who reflected the American way of life. There were no Maronite churches in the places where the Simons lived, and, as a result, they and many of their descendants became communicants in the Latin Rite of the Catholic Church. Some chose other denominations. By the end of the twentieth century there was little if any discernable social differences between the Simon descendants and most other Americans. Their assimilation was complete.

Aziz and Artie eventually divorced. He was working at the American Hat Company at the time of his death in 1947. He was fifty-three years old. Artie died in 1997 at age 90. During the late 1940s, Johnny finally found his music career unfulfilling and left it altogether. After completing a correspondence course, he opened his own television sales and service store in Green Cove Springs, Florida where he lived until his death in 1966 at age 69. After his death, Bessie, a widow when she married Johnny, moved to New Rochelle, New York and lived with a daughter from her first marriage. She was 89 when she died in 1986. In Jacksonville, Sy remained in the electrical businesses. When he died in 1984 at 83 he was still operating his own shop where he machined special carbon brushes for DC electric motors used aboard ships. Addie was 93 when she died in 1991. For the most part, George stayed in the electrical business operating as an electrical contractor. He and Helen eventually divorced, and, after his retirement, he returned to Montgomery where he lived until 1988. He was 75 at the time of his death. Helen died in 1998. She was 86. Frances outlived all her siblings. She and John Miaoulis divorced in the early 1950s, and he returned to Greece where he died in 1974 at age 72. Frances continued working for the State of Alabama Agricultural Department until her retirement. She died in 1996 when she was 85.

Frances Simon Miaoulis 1951

The legacy of Mary and Zaki Azar is remembered by many of those who knew them or who have heard of them. Not only were they loving and charitable to their immediate and extended families, they accepted the task of being surrogate parents to other children. George Farshee had great affection and respect for his oldest sister as did others who knew her for the good-hearted person she was. She passed away in 1960 at age 66. As for George's esteem for Zaki, he always addressed him as "Pop." When asked about his use of this paternal metaphor, George explained that at the time Zaki and Mary married, he, George, was two years old. Zaki had been a part of his life from almost its beginning. At the time of Badawi Simon's death in 1924, George was twelve years old. In the midst of grief and uncertainty, George continued, Zaki stepped forward and filled the economic void. He took it upon himself to see that Catherine Simon and her children had all the necessities of life. But helping financially support his mother-in-law and her children was only one facet of Zaki Azar. The personal qualities of this unequaled noble man included modesty, morality in personal and business matters, a spirited work ethic, dedication to his family, and an abiding concern for the wellbeing of others. He died in 1962 at age 72.[1]

THE END

Notes

Prologue: Friday, November 14, 1924

[1] Farshee, George (1982); Farshee, William (2006); Miaoulis (1982); November 15 and 16, *Montgomery Advertiser* (1924); death certificate (State of Alabama Bureau of Vital Statistics File No. 24448).

[2] Miaoulis (1982).

[3] Ibid. The cause of Badawi Simon's death listed on his death certificate was acute myocardis, inflammation of the heart muscle. There is no statement affirming than an autopsy was performed. According to Kay L. Donaldson, R.N. a member of the Providence Saint Vincent Medical Center cardiac surgical staff in Portland, Oregon, acute myocardis is detectable only by biopsy or an autopsy. Biopsies were not performed in 1924, and, in the absence of an autopsy, the cause of Badawi Simon's death as it appears on the death certificate is debatable.

As time passed after Badawi Simon's death several legends emerged. One was that the lunch at the Azar's was "heavy." This was in the days prior to the Vatican II reforms and because it was a Friday no meat would have been served. "Heavy" was never clearly defined. Another story is that around the time Badawi Simon departed the Azar home a dog was heard howling. In Arabic culture this is interpreted as the omen of an ominous event.

[4] The Zgharta accent is said to be attributable to Syriac, the language spoken in parts of North Lebanon until the Sixteenth and Seventeenth centuries.

[5] Farchakh, Semaan (n.d.).

Ehden, Zgharta and Religious Heritage

[1] The history of Ehden is from Dib (1962) and Hitti (1957).

[2] The description of contemporary Ehden is based upon the author's observations.

[3] The story of the nobleman and the people of Ehden is a traditional one. The account of the people of Ehden and Zgharta living in their two villages according to the season of the year is from (Goudard and Jalabert); (Hitti 1957), et al.

Old Names and New Names

[1] The origin of surnames and the example "ana Louis Ahl…" is from (Hitti 1957). The story of Badawi Ahl, the names of his descendents and the emergence of the Farchakh surname is from (Farchakh 1968, 1981). For the source of the history of the Tarek family see (Farchakh, Paul 1982).

[2] Forshee (1981).

[3] Badawi Simon Bible (n.d.).

[4] Farchakh, Paul (1982).

[5] Forshee (1981).

Badawi and Catherine

[1] Goudard & Jalabert (1966); Harik (1968).

[2] Miaoulis (1982).

[3] Farchakh, Boutros (1982).

[4] Forshee (1981), recounting stories told by Katherine Shakra.

[5] Miaoulis (1982).

[6] Forshee (1981). During a trip to the Cedars of Lebanon in 1982, the author met an elderly lady who recalled from her youth the log through which "holy water" flowed. In addition to their pilgrimage to the Cedars, George Farshee said that his parents also made a pilgrimage to Jerusalem. He cherished a small stone he said his mother had brought from Golgotha. This story, however, could not be confirmed with any other source.

[7] Hourani (1991).

[8] Farchakh, Boutros (1982).

[9] Miaoulis (1982).

[10] Forshee (1981).

[11] Miaoulis (1982), et al.

The Old Country Family

[1] Farchakh, Semaan (n.d.).

[2] Farchakh, Boutros (1982).

[3] Frangieh (2008).

[4] Leon (n.d.)

[5] Lattof (1981).

[6] Forshee (1981) and Miaoulis (1982) told to them by Katherine Shakra.

[7] Bey pronounced like the verb "bake" is an honorific title of Turkish origin similar in meaning to the English title Lord and the Italian title Don.

[8] Farchakh, Boutros (1982).

[9] Betts (1988), et al.

[10] Khalaf (2002).

[11] Traboulsi (2007).

[12] Goudard & Jalabert (1966) 220.

[13] Forshee (1981) and Miaoulis (1982), told to them by Badawi Simon.

[14] Goudard & Jalabert (1966).

[15] Traboulsi (2007).

[16] Farchakh, Semaan (n.d.).

[17] Farchakh, Boutros (1982), Frangieh (2007), et al.

[18] Farchakh, Haouach (1985).

[19] Khater (2001).

[20] Hawie (1981), Frangieh (2008), et al.

Dynamics of Emigration

[1] Hourani (1991), 294.

[2] Khater (2001).

[3] Ibid.

[4] Harik (1987).

[5] Khater (2001); Naff (1985). On June 17, 1919 at the Paris Peace Conference, the Council of Ten "the most powerful body of the state's

representatives" issued the following response to Turkey's objections to Western anti-Turkish cultural bias. "History tells us of many Turkish successes and many Turkish defeats…Yet in all these changes there is no case to be found, either in Europe or Asia or Africa, in which the establishment of Turkish rule in any country has not been followed by a diminution of material prosperity and a fall in the level of culture, nor is there any case to be found in which the withdrawal of Turkish rule has not been followed by a growth in material prosperity and a rise in the level of culture. Neither among the Christians nor among the Moslems…has the Turk done other than destroy whatever he has conquered." (Akcam 2006) 212-213.

[6] Farchakh, Boutros (1982).

[7] Antonius (1938).

[8] Tibari (1969).

[9] Khalaf (2002).

[10] Ibid.

[11] Tibari (1969).

[12] Ibid.; Hitti (1951) Vol. 2.

[13] Davison (1968) 39-40.

[14] Tibari (1969).

The Immigrant Experience and the Simon's First Emigration

[1] Hourani (1991); Khater (2001); Naff (1985); and Vincent- Barwood (1986).

[2] Ibid.

[3] Department of Commerce– Bureau of the Census 1910.

[4] Vincent-Barwood (1986).

[5] Hanania (1998).

[6] Higham (2004). In addition to Ellis Island, immigrants entered the US through the ports of New Orleans, Boston, Philadelphia, Providence and Baltimore.

[7] Naff (1985).

[8] Ibid.

[9] Farchakh, Semaan (n.d.)

[10] Maalouf (2004).

[11] Diaz de Kuri and Macluf (1995).

[12] Badawi Simon (1893).

[13] Twelfth Census of the United States (1900).

[14] Higham (2004) 3.

[15] Quoted in Higham (2004) 3.

[16] Higham (2004).

[17] Ibid.

[18] Higham (2004) 100.

[19] Higham (2004) 88.

[20] Higham (2004).

[21] Ibid.

[22] Naff (1985).

[23] Flynt (2004).

[24] Harik (1987).

[25] Farchakh, Boutros (1982).

[26] Naff (1985).

[27] Hitti (1924) 70; Naff (1985).

[28] Miaoulis (1982).

[29] Farchakh (1982).

[30] Badawi Simon (1892).

[31] Farchakh, Boutros 1982).

[32] Forshee (1981).

[33] Badawi Simon (1893).

[34] Ibid.

[35] Forshee (1981).

[36] Badawi Simon Bible (n.d.).

[37] Miaoulis (1982).

[38] Forshee (1981).

[39] Ibid.

[40] Miaoulis (1982).

[41] Ibid.

[42] Badawi Simon Bible (n.d.).

[43] Lattof (1981).

[44] Forshee (1981).

[45] Ibid., Farchakh, Boutros (1982).

[46] Ibid.

[47] Forshee (1981).

A New Home in America: Mobile

[1] Flynt (2004), Van der Veer(1984), and Woodward (1951).

[2] Ibid.

[3] Twelfth Census of the United States (1900).

[4] Ibid.

[5] Forshee (1981).

[6] Miaoulis (1982).

[7] Lattof (1981).

[8] Hawie (1981).

[9] Ibid.

[10] Forshee (1981).

[11] Ibid.

[12] Badawi Simon Bible (n.d.).

[13] Ibid.

[14] Forshee (1981).

[15] Ibid.

[16] Hawie, Wadih (1981).

[17] Miaoulis (1982).

[18] Towne et al (1895).

[19] State of Alabama (1904).

[20] Flynt (2004).

[21] Forshee (1981).

[22] Ibid.

[23] Forshee (1981); Hawie (1981).

[24] Miaoulis (1982).

[25] Pacific Wireless Telegraph Stock Certificate Number 6300 (1906).

[26] Electrical Review and Western Electrician (1910).

[27] Naff (1985).

[28] Amalgamated Association of Street and Railway Employees of America membership certificate (1907).

[29] Hawie, Wadih (1981); Miaoulis (1982).

[30] Ibid.

[31] Lattof (1981).

[32] Forshee (1981).

[33] Ibid.

[34] Forshee (1981); Miaoulis (1982).

[35] Forshee (1981).

[36] Miaoulis (1982).

[37] Forshee (1981).

[38] Lattof (1981). The year of Faris and Nazha's marriage (1906) is from Department of Commerce – Bureau of the Census (1910).

[39] Stauter (1981).

[40] Ibid.

[41] World War I Selective Service Draft Registration Cards (1917-1918).

[42] Stauter (1981).

[43] State of Alabama Center for Health Statistics (1924).

[44] Stauter (1981).

[45] Ibid.

[46] Ibid.

[47] Brothers of the Sacred Heart (1946).

Birmingham and Katherine Shakra

[1] Department of Commerce – Bureau of the Census (1910).

[2] Saint Elias Maronite Church Records.

[3] Department of Commerce – Bureau of the Census (1910).

[4] Forshee (1981).

[5] Details pertaining to a nephrectomy surgical procedure was provided by Sara DeHart Ph.D, associate professor Emeritus of Nursing, the University of Minnesota and Kay L. Donaldson, RN, Providence Saint Vincent Medical Center, Portland, Oregon.

[6] World War I Selective Service Draft Registration Cards (1917 – 1918); Department of Commerce – Bureau of the Census (1920).

[7] Forshee (1981); Miaoulis (1982).

[8] Miaoulis (1982).

[9] Ibid.

[10] Twelfth Census of the United States (1900).

[11] Forshee (1981).

[12] Miaoulis (1982).

[13] Department of Commerce - Bureau of the Census (1910).

Montgomery

[1] Neely (2006).

[2] Miaoulis (1982); Badawi Simon Bible (n.d.).

[3] Miaoulis (1982).

[4] Badawi Simon Bible (n.d.).

[5] Ibid.

[6] In her commentary on names, Naff (1985) 202-203 wrote that "Many of the [early Syrians] Anglicized their first and/or last names or accepted,

without complaint, their Anglicization by American bureaucrats (immigration officers and clerks who handled applications for naturalization papers, visas, passports, licenses, and other documents). They did not so much wish to disguise their ethnic identity as to overcome the difficulties of spelling and pronouncing Arabic sounds that are alien to Americans."

Zaki Azar and The American Hat Company

[1] McElvy (2005).

[2] Farshee, George (1982); Miaoulis (1982); Pappanastos (2007).

[3] Azar (1984).

[4] McElvy (2005).

[5] Home addresses and places of employment are from Montgomery City Directories (1912-1914).

[6] City Directory, Montgomery (1916-1917).

[7] Pappanastos (2007).

[8] World War I Selective Service Draft Registration Cards (1917-1918).

[9] City Directory, Montgomery (1916-1917).

[10] American Hat Company Transaction Agreement (1919).

[11] Farwell (1999) 124-125.

[12] City Directory, Montgomery (1916-1917).

[13] American Hat Company Transaction Agreement (1919).

Rheumatism, a Restaurant Venture and a New Career

[1] Wood (1913).

[2] State of Alabama Montgomery Court (1913).

[3] Forshee (1981).

[4] Department of Commerce - Bureau of the Census (1910).

[5] Miaoulis (1982).

[6] Conner (n.d.).

[7] Miaoulis (1982).

[8] Department of Commerce – Bureau of the Census (1920).

[9] Forshee (1981); Miaoulis (1982).

[10] Smith (1981).

[11] Cogburn (1916).

[12] Forshee (1981).

[13] Ibid.

[14] Ibid.

[15] Forshee (1981).

[16] Ibid.

[17] Farshee, William (2006).

[18] Farshee, Lori (1981).

The Great War

[1] Millis (1935).

[2] Khalaf (2002).

[3] The Gallipoli Campaign was launched in April 1915. Fighting was ferocious and the Ottoman Army under the command of German officers proved to be as murderously efficient with their Maxim machine guns as their German counterparts on the Western Front. In a matter of weeks, the bleeding on the Western Front was duplicated at Gallipoli as it too became bogged down in trench warfare. In early January 1916, barely nine months after being launched, the Allied expeditionary forces abandoned Gallipoli and withdrew under cover of darkness over a period of several nights. The official casualty figure for men from Great Britain, Australia, New Zealand and France totaled 252,000. Ottoman casualties were placed at 251,309 (Moorehead (1997). The Allied attack on Gallipoli coincided with an acceleration of the ongoing conflict between the Armenians of Anatolia and the Ottoman government. There were many massacres and major migrations of Armenians fleeing or driven out of Anatolia in what has become termed the Armenian genocide. Those who escaped went to neighboring countries. The influx of the Armenians exiles into Syria and Lebanon increased the need for food and humanitarian supplies on a population that was already in dire circumstances.

[4] Traboulsi (2007).

[5] Hall (2000).

[6] Farchakh, Boutros (1982).

[7] Zamir (1997).

[8] Quoted in Hawie, Ashad (1942) 75.

[9] Farchakh, Boutros (1982).

[10] Frangieh (2008).

[11] Farchakh, Paul (1981).

[12] Hawie, Wadih (1981).

[13] Farchakh, Paul (1981).

[14] Hall (2000).

[15] Frangieh (2008).

Syrian Americans Go to War

[1] Millis (1935).

[2] Ibid.

[3] Miaoulis (1982).

[4] Alabama National Guard Form 21 (n.d.).

[5] Millis (1935).

[6] Ibid.

[7] World War I Selective Service Draft Registration Cards (1917-1918).

[8] Slacker, in the context of World War I patriotic discourse usually referred to one who failed to register for the draft.

[9] Farwell (1999).

[10] Ibid.

[11] Graham (2005).

[12] Hawie, Wadih (1981).

[13] Ibid.

[14] Alabama National Guard Form 23 (n.d.).

[15] Hawie, Ashad (1942).

[16] Ibid.

[17] Ibid.

[18] World War I Selective Service Draft Registration Cards (1917-1918).

[19] Farshee, William (2006); Statement of Service (GSA Form 685) (n.d.).

[20] Farshee, William (2006).

[21] Flynt (2004).

[22] "Birmingham Man Dies From Wounds" (1918), Howard (1981), World War I Selective Service Draft Registration (1917-1918).

[23] Hawie, Wadih (1981).

[24] "Birmingham Man Dies From Wounds" (1918); "Syrian Dead To Be Honored Here – Colony Will Hold Annual Memorial Services for Michael Zataney" (1918).

[25] Ibid.

[26] Miaoulis (1982).

[27] Johnson (1919).

[28] Forshee (1981).

[29] Alabama National Guard Form No. 21 (n.d.).

[30] Johnson (1919).

[31] Ibid.

[32] Hawie, Ashad (1942).

[33] Farshee, William B. (2006).

[34] Perisco (2005).

[35] Johnson (1919).

[36] Meisenheimer, Robert L. (1981). National Personnel Records Center (GSA Form 7093). In succeeding years when the story of Michael Zataney was told it was said that he was killed after the Armistice went into effect at 11:00 a.m. on November 11, 1918. There is nothing in his military record to indicate the time of day he was killed but it is a fact that fighting did not immediately end at 11:00 a.m.(Johnson 1919). How Katherine Shakra might have learned the details of her son's death is not known but there were members of the 321st Infantry Regiment who lived in Birmingham, who knew Katherine Shakra and participated with her in various memorial services for fallen soldiers. Reconstructing the details of Michael Zataney's death or any soldier killed in battle can be difficult if not nearly impossible. Official records might be confusing especially when there are two slightly different versions as there is in this case. According to the Alabama Department of Archives and History Private Zataney was "killed in action" (Howard 1981). This version of his record makes no other comment or provide any details pertaining to his death.. His military record in The National Personnel Records center in St. Louis is slightly different. It states that he "died from wounds received in action on November 11, 1918 and buried November 14 in the AEF Cemetery 548" at Ancemont (Meisenheimer 1981). If the St. Louis record is accurate it is reasonable to surmise that Private Zataney did not die immediately from his wounds at whatever hour they were inflicted but was still alive when he was removed from the battlefield for transport to the field hospital at Ancemont. He evidently died while in transit or after he arrived there. Whichever occurred would account

for the location of his burial at the nearby Ancemont cemetery rather than one of the other temporary AEF cemeteries.

[37] Perisco (2005).

[38] "Syrian Dead to Be Honored Here" (1918).

[39] Higham (2004) 216.

[40] Hawie, Ashad (1942); "Rites Slated For Hero of World War I" (1962).

[41] Hitti (1924) 102-103.

[42] Ibid.

[43] Graham (2005). There were several reasons for the overseas burials which are explained in Chapter 2.

[44] American Memorials and Overseas Cemeteries (1980) published by The American Battle Monuments Commission.

[45] Ryan (1981).

[46] Graham (2005).

[47] "Local Death Mrs Shakra" (1961).

[48] Ibid.

112 South Bainbridge

[1] Azar, Edward (2008).

[2] World War I Selective Service Draft Registration Cards (1917-1918).

[3] Azar, Edward (2008).

[4] With the exception of cited entries, the description of 112 South Bainbridge and the events that occurred there are the author's.

[5] Pappanastos (2007).

[6] Farshee, William (2006).

[7] Farshee, Mary Catherine (2006).

[8] Forshee (1981).

The Roaring Twenties

[1] Naff (1985).

[2] King (2002).

[3] Hitti (1924) 89.

[4] Naff (1985).

[5] Bill of Sale (1920); Mortgage Document (1911).

[6] Ibid.

[7] Ibid.

[8] Farshee, George (1982).

[9] Miaoulis (1982).

[10] Forshee (1981).

[11] Ibid.

John B. Simon a.k.a. John B. Farshee

[1] Forshee (1981); Miaoulis (1982).

[2] Ibid.

[3] Elizabeth (Mrs R.D.) Johnson 1851-1935 (n.d.).

[4] Forshee (1981).

[5] Benjamin (1998).

[6] Farshee, George (1982).

[7] Miaoulis (1982).

[8] Department of Commerce – Bureau of the Census (1920).

[9] Forshee (1981).

[10] State of Ohio Bureau of Vital Statistics (1921).

[11] DeHart (2006).

[12] Forshee (1981); Miaoulis (1982).

[13] Fraunfelter, M.D., James (n.d.).

[14] State of Ohio Bureau of Vital Statistics (1921).

[15] Miaoulis (1982).

[16] State of Ohio Bureau of Vital Statistics (1921).

[17] "Dies at Hospital" (1921).

[18] Studwell et al (1999).

[19] Forshee (1981). The make of the automobile according so some other sources was a Model T Ford.

[20] Farchakh, Angele (2004).

[21] Farchakh, Rumanos (1921).

[22] Farchakh, Boutros (1982).

[23] Brahim (1982).

Alabama – The Early 1920s

[1] Forshee (1981).

[2] Ibid.

[3] Ibid.

[4] 721 Washington Avenue, Montgomery; Mortgage Document (1911).

[5] Miaoulis (1982).

[6] Ibid.

[7] Miaoulis (1982).

[8] Ibid.

[9] Farshee, George (1982).

[10] Farshee, George (1982); Miaoulis (1982).

[11] Farchakh-Bajjaly (2007).

[12] Miaoulis (1982).

[13] Ibid.

[14] Forshee (1981).

[15] Miaoulis (1982).

[16] Ibid.

Tragedy, Orlando, a Marriage and another Emigration

[1] Pappanastos (2007).

[2] Alabama Center for Health Statistics (1925).

[3] Farshee, Mary Catherine (2006).

[4] Miaoulis (1982).

[5] Pappanastos (2007).

[6] Miaoulis (1982).

[7] City Directory, Orlando, Florida (1926-1927).

[8] Ibid.

[9] "Florida Land Boom" internet article (2002).

[10] Miaoulis (1982).

[11] City Directory, Orlando, Florida (1925-1926).

[12] Farshee, Mary Catherine (2006); Farshee, William (2006).

[13] Zamir (1997).

[14] Ibid.

[15] Ibid.

[16] Farchakh, Angele (2004).

[17] Forshee (1981).

[18] Hitti (1924).

George Simon's Mobile Years

[1] Miaoulis (1982).

[2] Forshee (1981).

[3] Miaoulis (1982).

[4] Forshee (1981); Miaoulis (1982).

[5] Miaoulis (1982).

[6] Pappanastos (2007).

[7] Farshee, George (1982).

[8] Ibid.

[9] Brothers of the Sacred Heart (1946).

[10] Stauter (1981).

[11] Brothers of the Sacred Heart (1947).

[12] Farshee, George (1982).

[13] Ibid.

[14] Forshee (1981).

[15] Farshee, George (1982).

The Great Depression and Catherine Simon's Last Years

[1] Burg (2005).

[2] Clark (2008).

[3] Pappanastos (2007).

[4] Clark (2008).

[5] Farshee, William (2007).

[6] Miaoulis (1982).

[7] Ibid. Youssef Semaan Farchakh is seated on the left, Rumanos Semaan Farchakh on the right. Standing behind Youssef is his second son, Bakkos. Next to Bakkos is Boulos Sarkis Farchakh, son of Sarkis Semaan Farchakh.

[8] Ibid.

[9] Forshee (1981).

[10] Farshee, George (1982); Forshee (1981); Miaoulis (1982). Each provided a version of the story.

[11] Hitti (1924).

[12] Miaoulis (1982).

[13] Farshee, George (1982); Forshee (1981); Miaoulis (1982).

[14] Brahim (1981).

[15] Forshee (1981).

[16] Hawie (1981).

[17] Forshee (1981).

[18] Brahim (1982).

[19] Farchakh, Angele (2004).

[20] Ibid.

[21] Farchakh, Paul (2008).

[22] Miaoulis (1982).

[23] Pappanastos (2007).

[24] Farshee, Helen (1982).

[25] Ibid.

[26] Miaoulis (1982).

[27] Farshee (1982); Forshee (1981); Miaoulis (1982).

[28] Forshee (1981); Miaoulis (1982).

[29] Forshee (1981).

[30] Miaoulis (1982).

[31] Forshee (1981).

[32] Farshee, Helen (1982).

[33] Miaoulis (1982).

[34] Alabama Center for Health Statistics File No. 28587 (1938).

[35] Ibid.

[36] "Mrs. Catherine Farshee" (1938).

[37] Miaoulis (1982).

[38] Census reports for 1900, 1910, 1920, 1930 list Catherine Simon's birth year as 1874 or her age which would have placed her birth in that year.

The Way of the Emigrants: For Better or Worse

[1] On May 3, 1962, three days after Zaki Azar's death, the following eulogy appeared on the editorial page of the *Alabama Journal*:

> The death of Mr. Zaki N. Azar removes one of Montgomery's most remarkable citizens. He was a conspicuous example of the opportunities that a city like Montgomery affords a man from abroad, and the successful seizure of those opportunities.
>
> He was a native of Antioch, that region of the Levantine coast of the eastern Mediterranean which has produced so many men of historic prominence. Mr. Azar came to Montgomery as a youth more than fifty years ago with a bare minimum of formal schooling. In the half century of his residence here he built a successful business; he reared a fine family of eleven children, five sons and six daughters.
>
> The relationship between Mr. Azar and his children was a beautiful thing to see. To them he was as a patriarch of old whose word was law, and to them he was also a most affectionate and devoted parent. Most of the children have had some experience in the Azar store called the American Hat Company, though it had gradually become a store handling all sorts of clothing and supplies for men.
>
> To his daughters he showed his devotion on all occasions. When any of them visited the store he could be seen greeting them affectionately and then escorting them to the door with his arms around their shoulders.
>
> For many months Mr. Azar had not been in good health and recently had to forego his walks to and from his home on Bainbridge Street. He was a fine, upright, modest, sincere and devoted citizen and loyal friend to those he liked. Mr. Azar was a unique figure in Montgomery's business and fraternal and church life. It is rare that we meet his like in these days of complex and fast living with little time for cultivating the finer things of life.

Bibliography

Primary Sources

Alabama Center for Health Statistics. Certificate of Death Joe N. Azar. File No. 9551 April 1, 1925.

Alabama Center for Health Statistics. Certificate of Death Catherine Simon Farshee. File No. 28587 December 28, 1938.

Alabama National Guard Form No. 21. .n.d.* Military service record of John Simon (John B. Farshee) Service number 1350087.

Alabama National Guard Form No. 23. n.d. Military service record of Wadih Farris Hawie Service number 1727735.

Amalgamated Association of Street and Electric Railway Employes (*sic*) of America Certificate of Membership 1907.

American Hat Company. 1919 Transaction agreement for purchase of American Hat Company by Zaki Azar from Joe Toronto. February 5.

Azar, Edward J. 2008. Letter to author.

Azar, Gabi. 1984 Letter to Edward J. Azar concerning Azar relatives in Syria and Lebanon. January 10. Letter provided to author by Edward J. Azar.

Bill of Sale between sellers J.F. and Mattie Morgan and purchaser B. Simon for home at 723 Washington Avenue, Montgomery, Alabama. July 12, 1920.

Brahim, Maron. 1982 Tape recorded interview with author. Puebla, Mexico. Week of January 24.

C.D. Spiker Funeral Parlor. Canton, Ohio. Archives.

Clark, Edward P. 2008. Interview with author Montgomery, Alabama March 20.

Cogburn, Dr. H.R. 1916. "To Whom It May Concern" letter "certifying" Dr. B. Simon as a competent optician. June 20.

Department of Commerce – 1900 Census. *See Twelfth Census.*

Department of Commerce - Bureau of the Census: Thirteenth Census of the United States: 1910-Population.

Department of Commerce - Bureau of the Census: Fourteenth Census of the United States: 1920-Population.

Department of Commerce – Bureau of the Census: Fifteenth Census of the United States: 1930 Population Schedule.

Donaldson, Kay L. 2008. Interview with author Beaverton, Oregon January 18 and other dates.

DeHart, Sara S. 2006. Telephone interview with author May 15 and other dates.

Document of land sale between Butrous Sarkis Farchakh and Rumanos Semaan Farchakh 1926.

Farchakh, Angele Sarkis Youssef. 2004. Interviews with author. Ehden, Lebanon. Various dates July and August.

Farchakh, Badawi Semaan. n.d. *Bible.* Entries made by Badawi Simon on pages reserved for births, marriages and deaths. Translated from Arabic by Paul Mkhayel Farchakh.

———. 1892 Letter from Badawi Semaan Farchakh in Mobile, Alabama to his father Semaan Mkhayel Farchakh in Zgharta. March 13. Translated from Arabic by Paul Mkhayel Farchakh.

———. 1893 Letter from Badawi Semaan Farchakh in Tampa-St. Petersburg, Florida to his brother, Sarkis Semaan Farchakh in Merida, Mexico. Letter addressed to Santiago Simon (a.k.a. Sarkis Semaan). Translated from Arabic by Paul Mkhayel Farchakh.

Farchakh, Boutros Sarkis. 1968. Letter to Said Badawi Farchakh (Sy Forshee). April. 21.

———. 1970. Letter to Said Badawi Farchakh (Sy Forshee). N.D.

———. 1981. Letter to author. Translated into English by Mary Rose Frangieh. N.D.

_____. 1982. Interview with author. Zgharta, Lebanon various dates November.

Farchakh, Haouach Sarkis. 1985. Letter to author. March 15.

———. 1985. Letter to author. November 18.

Farchakh, Paul Mkhayel. 1981. Interview with author. Los Angeles, California. May 2. Also Albuquerque, New Mexico; Fort Worth, Texas; Zouk and Ehden, Lebanon various dates.

———. 1981. Recorded interview with his paternal grandparents Boutros Sarkis Farchakh and Mareen Nakad Farchakh, Zgharta. September.

Farchakh, Paul Mkhayel with Angele and Mkhayel Farchakh. 1984. Interview with author Albuquerque, New Mexico. July 14.

Farchakh, Romanus Semaan. 1921. Letter to his sister Nazha Farchakh Hawie written from Detroit, Michigan confirming his and his family's forthcoming departure for Lebanon. May 2. Translated from Arabic by Paul Mkhayel Farchakh.

Farchakh, Said Badawi. *See Sy Forshee.*

Farchakh, Semaan Mkhayel. n.d. *Personal Journal.* Information from this document provided by George S. Farchakh, Paris, France.

Farchakh, Georges S. 1981. Letter to author. May 10.

———. 1982. Interviews with author. Mexico City. Week of January 24.

———. 1982. Interview with author. Paris, France. October 23.

———. 1983. Letter to author. March 8.

———. 1988. Interview with author. Paris, France. November 7.

Farshee, George B. 1982. Interview with author May 15 and other dates.

Farshee, Helen Boone. 1982. Tape recorded interview with author January 4 Albuquerque, New Mexico. Telephone and in person interviews various dates.

Farshee, Lori Ann. 1981. Data from Alabama Department of Archives and History and information from St. Peter's Catholic Church records. Letter to author. June 2.

———. 2006. "Doc info." Biographical information on Sim B. Farshee grandfather of Lori Ann Farshee. Email to author. April 6.

Farshee, Mary Catherine. 2006. Telephone interview with author. August 7 and various other dates.

Farshee, William B. 2006. Interview with author, Montgomery, Alabama, December 3 and other dates.

Forshee, Addie Smith. 1981. Interview with author, Jacksonville, Florida, October 11.

Forshee, Sy. 1980. Interview with author, Montgomery, Alabama. July; October 11, 1981. Jacksonville, Florida and other dates.

Frangieh, Helene Farchakh. 2008. Interview with author, Zgharta, Lebanon. September 18 and other dates.

General Services Administration, National Personal Records Center, Military Personnel Records. 1981. Letter to author providing details of Michael Assad Zataney's death on Armistice Day 1918. June 23.

Hawie, Ashad G. 1942. *The Rainbow Ends.* New York: Theo. Gaus' Sons.

Hawie, Wadih F. 1981. Interview with author, Mobile, Alabama. April 8.

Howard, Milo B. 1981. Letter to Douglas McElvy from State of Alabama Department of Achieves and History providing military service record of Michael Assad Zataney Service number 3206670. July 22. Letter provided to author by Douglas McElvy.

Kassouf, Naomi Hawie. 1981. Interview with author. Birmingham, Alabama. April 10.

Lattof, Catherine Leon. 1981. Interview with author. Mobile, Alabama. April 8. (Note: Lattof was adopted in place of Ltayf).

——. 1981. Letter to author. June 30.

Leon, George. n.d. Unpublished notes provided to author by George Leon's cousin, Catherine Leon Latoff. 1980.

McElvy, Douglas. 2005. Letter (with documents) providing details of his maternal grandfather's (Zaki Azar) birth and US arrival record. Letter to author. October 4.

Meisenheimer. Robert L. 1981. "Zataney, Michael A. 3206670." GSA Form 7093 providing details of Michael Zataney's temporary burial site. National Personnel Records Center, St. Louis. June 23.

Miaoulis, Frances Simon. 1982. Tape recorded interview with author January 3 Albuquerque, New Mexico. Telephone and in-person interviews with author various dates.

Mortgage Document for home at 723 Washington Avenue, Montgomery, Alabama. United States Mortgage and Trust Company, New York. 1911.

Nakad, Mareen. 1982. Tape recorded interview with author. Puebla, Mexico. Week of January 24.

Pacific Wireless Telegraph Company Stock Certificate # 6300 dated December 20, 1906 issued to Badawi Simon.

Pappanastos. Dodie Azar. 2007. Correspondence with author. April 2. Interview December 3, 2006 and other dates.

Ryan, Jr., Colonel William E. 1981. Letter to author from American Battle Monuments Commission providing name of burial site of Michael Assad Zataney. July 13.

Saint Elias Maronite Church, Birmingham, Alabama. Church records.

Saint John's Episcopal Church, Mobile, Alabama. Church records.

Saint Peter's Catholic Church, Montgomery, Alabama. Church records.

Simon, Badawi. *See Badawi Semaan Farchakh.*

Smith, Willard. 1981. Letter to Edward J. Azar explaining the history of the State of Alabama regulation of optometrists. July 10. Letter provided to author by Edward J. Azar.

State of Alabama. 1904. License issued to B. Simon to transact business as a peddler with wagon drawn by one horse or other animal in Baldwin County. January 9.

————. 1905. License issued to B. Simon to transact business as a peddler with wagon drawn by one horse or another animal in Baldwin County. January 17.

State of Alabama Center for Health Statistics. Certificate of Death Mansour Jabbour Leon File No. 18170 August 26, 1924.

State of Alabama Bureau of Vital Statistics. Certificate of Death B. Simon Farschee (*sic*) File No. 24448 November 19, 1924.

State of Alabama Montgomery County. 1913. Judge of Probate J.B. Gaston certification that B. Simon is unable to perform manual labor and is authorized to peddle in any county in Alabama without a license. May 28.

State of Ohio Bureau of Vital Statistics. Certificate of Death Dora Farshee File No. 52779 November 17, 1921.

Statement of Service (GSA Form 6851) n.d. Military Personnel Records Center, St. Louis, Missouri. Military Service Record of Sim B. Farshee Service Number AR 653697.

Stauter, Annie Leon. 1981. Interviews and letters to author. Various dates.

Twelfth Census of the United States: Schedule No. 1 – Population [1900].

Wood, Dr. M.L. 1913. Certification from Montgomery County Board of Health that B. Simon suffers from chronic rheumatism and recommending he be granted a license to peddle. May 27.

World War I Selective Service Draft Registration Cards, 1917-1918. www.Ancestry.com 2006 - 2008.

Yammine, Mehsen. 1982. Interview with author, Zgharta. November 9.

Newspapers

"B. Simon Farshee." 1924. Obituary. *The Montgomery Advertiser*, November 16.

"Birmingham Man Dies From Wounds." 1918. Newspaper account of Michael Zataney's death. *The Birmingham News.* November 28.

Conner, Tom. "Remember When." *The Montgomery Advertiser* N.D. Clipping provided to author by Mary Ann Neeley.

"Death Comes To Mr. Azar." 1962. *Alabama Journal*, May 3.

"Dies at Hospital." 1921. Obituary of Dora Farshee. *Canton Repository* (Ohio). September 17.

"Dr. Barson Rounding Out 25 Years of Service in State." 1940. *The Montgomery Advertiser*, May 13.

"Falls Dead Over Steering Wheel: B. Simon Frashee (*sic*) Dies as He Enters Yard of Prospective Customer." 1924. *The Montgomery Advertiser*, November 15.

"Farshee, Simon B. (Dock)." 1947. Obituary. *Alabama Journal*. February 18.

"Hawie – Mrs. Nazha Farshee Hawie." 1946. Obituary. *The Birmingham News.* December 24.

"Joseph N. Azar." 1925. Obituary. *The Montgomery Advertiser.* April 2.

"Leon – Mrs. Selma Leon." 1942. Obituary. *Mobile Register.* November 16.

"Local Deaths Mrs. Shakra." 1961. Obituary. *The Birmingham News,* July 15.

"M.J. Leon." 1924. Obituary. *Mobile Register,* August 29.

"Mrs. Catherine Farshee." 1938. Catherine Simon Obituary. *The Montgomery Advertiser.* December 28.

"Postal Raids Show Vast Stock Frauds." 1910. *New York Times.* November 22. *www.nytimes.com.2007.*

"Rites Slated For Hero of World War I." 1962. Ashad G. Hawie Obituary. *Mobile Register.* September 14.

"Syrian Dead To Be Honored Here – Colony Will Hold Annual Memorial Services for Michael Zataney." 1918. *The Birmingham News.* December 2.

References

Akcam, Taner.2006. *A Shameful Act: The Armenian Genocide and the Question of Turkish Responsibility*. New York: Metropolitan Books.

American Memorials and Overseas Cemeteries (Pamphlet). 1980. Washington, DC: The American Battle Monuments Commission.

Antonius, George. 1938. *The Arab Awakening*. Beirut: Khayats.

Benjamin, Rick. 1998. "Arthur Pryor: Ragtime Pioneer." www.paragonragtime.com/pryor.html.

Betts, Robert Brenton. 1988. *The Druze*. New Haven: Yale University Press.

Brothers of the Sacred Heart. 1946. *A century of service for the Sacred Heart in the United States by the Brothers of the Sacred Heart, 1847-1947*.

Burg, David F. 2005. *The Great Depression, Updated Edition*. New York: Facts On File, Inc.

Chahine, Richard A. ed. 1997. *Lebanon: Pictures of our Heritage Fortified Dwellings and Religious Architecture Volume II*. Beirut: Richard A. Chahine.

City Directory, Birmingham, Alabama, various dates. Birmingham: R.L. Polk and Company.

City Directory, Canton, Ohio (publisher not known).

City Directory, Mobile, Alabama, various dates. Birmingham: R.L. Polk and Company.

City Directory, Montgomery, Alabama, various dates. Birmingham: R.L. Polk and Company.

City Directory, Orlando, Florida, 1926-1927. Jacksonville: R.L. Polk and Company.

Cowan, J.M. ed. 1994. *Arabic-English Dictionary: The Hans Wehr Dictionary of Modern Written Arabic* 4th ed. Ithaca, NY: Spoken Language Services, Inc.

Davison, Roderic H. 1968. *Turkey*. Englewood Cliffs, NJ: Prentice-Hall, Inc.

Dean, John W. 2004. *Warren G. Harding*. New York: Time Books.

DeHart Sara S. 2006. "Dora Moses." Email document provided to the author. December 31.

Diaz de Kuri, Martha and Lourdes Macluf. *From Lebanon to Mexico: chronicle of an emigrant people*. www.caza-zgharta.com.

Dib, Pierre. 1962. *History of the Maronite Church*. Detroit: Maronite Apostolic Exarchate. (Translated from the original French text by Seely Beggiani).

Electrical Review and Western Electrician. 1910. "Wireless Companies Consolidate." May 21, p. 1044. From internet website *Wireless Companies Consolidate (1910)*.

"Elizabeth (Mrs. R.D.) Johnston (1851-1934)." Alabama Women's Hall of Fame – Elizabeth Johnston. From Alabama Women's Hall of Fame website.

Farchakh-Bajjaly, Joanne. 2007. "Funeral Mourners." Email message to author. March 6.

Farchakh, Paul Mkhayel. 1982. Translation of excerpts from *History of Ehden Part III The History of the Families from Ehden*. Semaan El Khazen 1968 p. 319. N.D.

Farwell, Byron. 1999. *Over There: The United States in the Great War*. New York: W.W. Norton.

"Florida's Land Boom." 2002. Website: *Exploring Florida*; University of South Florida.

Flynt, Wayne. 2004. *Alabama in the Twentieth Century*. Tuscaloosa: The University of Alabama Press.

Fraunfelter M.D., James. www.heritagepursuit. com/Stark/ Stark01P117. htm.

Goudard, Joseph and Henri Jalabert. 1966. *Lebanon the Land and the Lady*. Beirut: The Catholic Press. Translated by Eugene P. Burns.

Graham, John W. 2005. *The Gold Star Mother Pilgrimages of the 1930s*. Jefferson NC: McFarland & Company, Inc., Publishers.

Hall, Loretta. 2000. *Arab American Voices*. Detroit: U-X-L

Hanania, Ray. 1998. Arabs on Titanic: "We Share the Pain But Not the Glory." Arab Media Service website April 8

Harik, Elsa Marston. 1987. *The Lebanese in America*. Minneapolis: Lerner Publishing Company

Harik, Iliya F. 1968. *Politics and Change in a Traditional Society – Lebanon 1711-1845*. Princeton: Princeton University Press.

Higham, John. 2004 (1955). *Strangers in the Land: Patterns of American Nativism, 1860-1925*. New Brunswick, NJ: Rutgers University Press.

Hitti, Philip K. 1924. *The Syrians in America*. Piscataway, NJ: Gorgias Press.

———. 1951. *History of Syria including Lebanon and Palestine* Vols. I and II. Piscataway, NJ: Gorgias Press.

———. 1957. *Lebanon in History*. New York: St. Martin's Press.

Hourani, Albert. 1991. *A History of the Arab Peoples*. New York: MJF Books.

Johnson, Clarence Walton. 1919. *The History of the 321st Infantry*. Columbia, SC: The R.L. Bryan Company.

Khalaf, Samir. 2002. *Civil and Uncivil Violence in Lebanon: A History of the Internationalization of Communal Conflict*. New York: Columbia University Press.

Khater, Akram Fouad. 2001. *Inventing Home; Emigration, Gender, and the Middle Class in Lebanon, 1870-1920.* Berkeley: University of California Press.

King, Desmond. 2002. *Making Americans – Immigration, Race, and the Origins of the Diverse Democracy*. Cambridge: Harvard University Press.

Maalouf, Amin. 2008. *Origins*. New York: Farrar, Straus and Giroux.

"Maronite Rite." 1967. *New Catholic Encyclopedia*. Washington, DC: The Catholic University of America.

McCarthy, Justin. 2001. *The Ottoman Peoples and the End of Empire*. New York: Oxford University Press.

Millis, Walter. 1935. *Road to War: America 1914-1917.* Boston: Houghton Mifflin Company.

Moorehead, Alan. 1997. *Gallipoli*. Hertfordshire, England: Wordsworth Editions Limited.

Moosa, Matti. 1986. *The Maronites in History*. Syracuse: Syracuse University Press.

Muskat, Beth Taylor and Mary Ann Neely. 1985. *The Way It Was 1850-1930: Photographs of Montgomery and Her Central Alabama Neighbors*. Montgomery: Landmarks Foundation of Montgomery.

Naff, Alexa. 1985. *Becoming American: The Early Arab Immigrant Experience*. Carbondale: Southern Illinois University Press.

Neeley, Mary Ann. 2006. "Pre-WWI Immigrants in Montgomery." Email to author, December 15.

Netton, Ian Richard. 1997. *A Popular Dictionary of Islam*. Chicago: NTC Publishing Group.

Persico, Joseph E. 2005. *Eleventh Month, Eleventh Day, Eleventh Hour: Armistice Day 1918 World War I and Its Violent Climax*. New York: Random House Trade Paperbacks.

Salibi, Kamal. 2003. *A House of Many Mansions: The History of Lebanon Reconsidered*. London: I.B. Tauris.

Studwell, William E., Charles P. Conrad, Bruce R. Schueneman. 1999. *Circus Songs-An Annotated Anthology*. New York: The Haworth Press.

Tibari, A.L. 1969. *A Modern History of Syria including Lebanon and Palestine*. London: Macmillan and Company, Ltd.

Towne, E.C., A.J. Canfield and George J. Hagar, eds. 1895. *Rays of Light from All Lands – The Bibles and Beliefs of Mankind*. New York: Gay Brothers & Company.

Traboulsi, Fawwaz. 2007. *A History of Modern Lebanon*. London: Pluto Press.

Van der Veer Hamilton, Virginia. 1984. *Alabama A History*. New York: W.W. Norton & Company.

Vincent-Barwood, Aileen. 1986. "The Arab Immigrants." *Aramco World Magazine*. September-October.

Woodward, C. Vann. 1951. *Origins of the New South 1877-1913*. Baton Rouge: Louisiana State University Press.

Zamir, Meir. 1997. *Lebanon's Quest: The Road to Statehood 1926-1939*. London: I.B. Tauris.

Asterisk (*) indicates No Date (n.d.)

Acknowledgements

In addition to those individuals and organizations listed in the bibliography I also extend my gratitude to others who provided information and documents and conducted research on my behalf: Zack Azar III, Michael Paul Farchakh, and Lee R. Gray. I owe Joanne Farchakh Bajjaly a special note of thanks. She provided answers to my many questions related to Lebanon's history and helped me understand certain Arabic linguistic structures. At various times I sought comments from others including Michel Kanaan, Samir Lakkees, and Aziz Shalaby, all immigrants from Lebanon and American citizens living in the Portland, Oregon area. I thank Jane Guzman, Ph.D, of Dallas, Texas who critiqued the first draft of the manuscript.

Through the Beaverton, Oregon Library interlibrary loan service, to which I extend my thanks, I gained access to books that were out of print and microfilm copies of a number of newspapers. The Alabama Department of Achieves and History and the Alabama Center for Health Statistics provided documents and other information. I am indebted to the Orange County Library Genealogical Section in Orlando, Florida as well as the Stark County, Ohio library in Canton.

I hope I have not omitted my thanks to anyone, but if I did it was due to oversight not ingratitude.

Louis Farshee
Beaverton, Oregon
2010

Index

Made in the USA
Lexington, KY
27 January 2016